We Have a Pope

We Have a Pope

a Portrait of His Holiness John XXIII

by Monsignor Albert Giovannetti
Auditor of the Vatican Secretariat of State

Translated from the Italian by
JOHN CHAPIN

THE NEWMAN PRESS • 1959 • *Westminster, Maryland*

Nihil Obstat: Edward A. Cerny, S.S., D.D.
Censor Librorum

Imprimatur: Francis P. Keough, D.D.
Archbishop of Baltimore

January 9, 1959

The *Nihil Obstat* and *Imprimatur* are official declarations that a book or pamphlet is free of doctrinal and moral error. No implication is contained therein that those who have granted the *Nihil Obstat* and *Imprimatur* agree with the opinions expressed.

Preface

two words: peace and prosperity. He spoke of this not only as spiritual head, but also as one of the people speaking with regard to its governors. This led him to recall the *solidarity* which ought to bind nations together and which corresponds to one of the fundamental aspirations of humanity.

The universality of spiritual, human, and civil values has been stressed and tied together in the first message of John XXIII. From this universality springs his appeal for the reconciliation of all the Christian Churches, and for the return of those "separated Churches" to the fold of Peter.

People have understood all this and therefore immediately come to love the new pope. John XXIII has already acquired a wide popularity in the world at large.

It is to be hoped that the separated Churches will especially respond to his appeal for unity and, as he has said, return to their own house.

It is to be hoped that all men of good will will unite themselves with believers around this voice, whom God has chosen to make His voice heard throughout the world.

And the voice of John XXIII will repeat to all men, as he has already repeated to the faithful in Venice: "The only way basically in which we can be good Christians is to do good."

Simple words, divinely simple, but words that will not pass away.

ALBERT GIOVANNETTI

Contents

✠ ✠ ✠

Contents

List of Illustrations

✠ ✠ ✠

John XXIII, *frontispiece*

Between pages 18 and 19

We Have a Pope

1. Bergamo and Rome

✠ ✠ ✠

A NGELO Giuseppe Roncalli was born on November 25, 1881 at a small place called Brusico, in the commune of Sotto il Monte, in the province and diocese of Bergamo.

This small commune in northern Italy, perched on a hill in a pleasant region dotted with vineyards, is situated about nine miles from Bergamo, between the last spurs of the Alps and the plain, near the Adda river. It numbers today about 2,000 inhabitants, but when the future supreme pontiff John XXIII was born, there were far fewer, and the life led was then truly patriarchal: no telegraph, no telephone, and only one road with very little traffic.

The houses still have preserved their primitive simplicity, modest country dwellings which contrast strangely with the few modern buildings erected after the war and the old former parish church of San Giovanni. A medieval structure which is gradually losing its stucco, this building

3

is always closed except on October 1, the feast day of the region, when it is open for Mass. The present parish church, which Archbishop Roncalli, then apostolic visitor in Bulgaria, consecrated in 1929, is located on a hill approached through an *allée* of cypresses, and is dedicated to the Mother of God.

But the one part of the community which preserves best the look of former years is the small cemetery, situated along the edge of the provincial road Ponte San Pietro-Calusco, in a quiet, secluded spot, approached by a pathway of nineteen steps bordered by clipped fir trees. There are few chapels and many stones here, simple stones with only the names and dates of the dead on them. The tombs of the Roncalli family are to be found grouped together in one of the far corners, on the right as one enters the cemetery.

Sotto il Monte belongs to one the best organized dioceses in Italy and has been traditionally devoted to the Church and its hierarchy. The clergy of Bergamo excel in zeal, learning, and a spirit of initiative in the fields of religious instruction, the press, and social activities. According to statistics, the diocese of Bergamo is the first in Italy for the number of vocations to the religious life and for priests generously placed at the disposal of other dioceses less fortunately supplied.

When Giuseppe Roncalli was asked, on the day after his brother's election as supreme pontiff, what he thought about seeing him as the new head of the Church, he replied: "With so many becoming priests here in Bergamo, one was bound to become pope!"

The inhabitants of the province of Bergamo are accustomed to emigrate to other countries, for the most part for seasonal work in Europe (and Nuncio Roncalli would find "his" Bergamasks practically everywhere and would always make much of the occasion). Those who remain behind are for the most part workers in the fields or small landholders, naturally humble and thrifty, conservative and attached to the existing order, even though compelled to lead a life of hard labor to earn a modest living.

HIS FAMILY

His parents, Giovanni Battista Roncalli and Marianna Mazzola, belonged to this class of humble and tenacious peasantry, bound to the soil, raising a large and healthy family, educating them to observe the Christian virtues, serenely content with their own lot.

Both were of sturdy stock (his father died on July 28, 1935, at 81 and his mother on February 20, 1939, at 84). There were ten children. Of these, the present supreme pontiff is the third child, but the first of the sons. All of them, with the exception of a sister who died at the age of 25, have lived to a ripe old age. Three brothers and a sister are still living today—they always use *"voi"* when speaking to Angelo—besides a raft of eighteen nephews and nieces, of whom one is curate at

Fusignano (in the province of Ravenna) and two are nuns (Sister Anna, a missionary in Asmara, and Sister Maria Angelica, a nurse in a hospital in Rome).[1]

The Roncalli family has lived on the same land for generations. It seems that they first came to Sotto il Monte in 1420, the year in which the founder of the family *"Martinus Roncalli dictus Maitinus"* moved there from Valle Imagna, "the most beautiful of the Lombard valleys," according to one authority.

Attempts have been made to link the origin of this family with that of other Roncallis in Bergamo and other towns in Italy, people who prospered and even attained noble rank, but John XXIII smiles at the zealous researchers who would claim such an illustrious background for him. Sufficient indication of what he thinks about all this may be gathered from the words which he addressed to the faithful at San Marco in Venice when he took possession there as patriarch: "I come from humble stock and I grew up in an atmosphere of self-sufficient blessed poverty, which makes few demands." After his election as pope when he was asked whether he wished the traditional designation of "Excellency" (*Eccellentissimi*) to be given to his brothers, he said that the title of "Relatives of John XXIII" would be sufficient.

[1] John XXIII's living brothers and sister are: Saverio, who is married but has no children; Alfredo, who never married; Giuseppe, a widower with five sons and five daughters; Assunta, the widow Marchesi, with four sons. In 1957 a younger brother Giovanni died, leaving eight sons.

Bergamo and Rome

His family used to live in an old house (torn down years ago and replaced by new owners) and then in a farmhouse, called Colombara, later Roncalli. His parents moved to this abode when little Angelo was only eight years old. Two of his brothers and some of his nephews have remained there, leading the same thrifty, peaceful existence they always have, devoting themselves to the cultivation of their land.

The Roncalli farmhouse, owned jointly by the surviving brothers (of whom one is the present pope), is also an old building of moderate size, well preserved and maintained. Painted yellow, it has a courtyard in front of red brick. On the wall, under the porch, is displayed the coat of arms of Angelo Roncalli as cardinal: a tower in an open field, with lilies, surmounted by the lion of San Marco, and at the bottom the motto *"Obœdientia et pax."* On the center wall there is a picture of Our Lady of Lourdes, surrounded by dahlias. On another part of the porch, more or less opposite the coat of arms, has been fastened a terracotta lion of San Marco. Inside there are a few rooms done in sixteenth-century country style, with simple, dignified, attractive furnishings.

From Colombara the eye wanders over the Lombard plain between the Adda and the Brembo, looking down toward Brianza. Somasca may be seen, sacred to the memory of St. Jerome Emiliani, whom the pope has always greatly admired from his early days as a priest; the shrine of *Madonna del Bosco,* crowned by the patriarch of

Venice on September 30, 1954; the abbey of Pontida; the Bergamask shrines of our Lady called the *"Madonna dei Campi,"* the *"Madonna della Cornabusa,"* and the *"Madonna delle Rose."*

During the last years of the nineteenth century the Roncalli household led a very frugal existence at Colombara. Meals were simple: in the morning, a little *semolino* (wheat meal) and a bit of *polenta;* at noon, some vegetable soup, with *formaggio* or stuffed meat; in the evening, usually the same type of meal. Wines and sweets were rarely served. "We were very poor," the pope recalled on the occasion of one of his visits to his native land, "but we were happy and we were not aware of lacking anything. In reality, we lacked nothing. Ours was a dignified, self-sufficient poverty."

HIS EARLY YEARS

Soon after his birth, in accordance with local custom, his parents, who were very pious, wished to have him baptized. But the parish priest was away, pastoral duties having summoned him to Terno, a nearby community. Hence the ceremony had to be put off until dusk. The newborn child was carried to the parish church, dedicated to St. John the Baptist, while the *tramontana* was blowing and cold autumnal rain swept the countryside and the roads were almost deserted.

Angelino grew strong in the free life of the fields. When he reached school age, he began to imbibe the first elements of knowledge at the elementary school in Sotto il Monte. At that time, there were only the first three grades and classes were all taught in one room. The boy showed that he could learn, and displayed a remarkable eagerness to do so and an exceptional memory. His brother Giuseppe and an old friend, Battista Agazzi, called Battistel, today recall those days. Agazzi was attending the third grade and Angelo the first. The teacher was named Donizetti (like the great Bergamask composer). Angelo Roncalli always sat on the first bench, which was the bench for the best students, while Agazzi was in the back of the room. "Roncalli who was in first grade knew more than we did who were in third grade," says Battistel. "We knew even then that he would become great some day." Agazzi has always been a good friend of Angelo Roncalli, who used to come to Sotto il Monte for his vacation regularly each summer, whether from Paris, Rome, or Venice, always stopping his car in front of the iron shop of his old companion of school days, and opening the door to ask: "How are you, Battistel?"

Much of his free time was spent by Angelino in the church of San Giovanni and in the fields, helping his father with his hard work. Angelo Roncalli will always remain "tied" to the soil. When in Bulgaria as apostolic delegate he made a systematic study of the agriculture of the country and took an interest in the life of the peasants (he made several trips to the stupendous "Valley of the Roses"); the life led there reminded him of that of his hard-working Bergamasks.

After finishing the first three grades of elementary school, the boy was enrolled in the episcopal college of Celana, near Bergamo, to continue his studies. At first he stayed with a relative who lived in Pontida, a short distance away from Celana; but after a few weeks the child came back home. From that time on, every day, he was obliged to make a long trip from Sotto il Monte to Celana and back again. The road was hard for one who went on foot, for there were no means of transportation in those days and a simple bicycle was too great a luxury for a family in such modest circumstances. Hence there were two hours of walking each morning and the same in the evening. These hikes were occasionally quite trying, especially in winter, when it gets quite cold in these sub-Alpine regions, even if they are in "sunny Italy."

While Angelino made good progress during the first three years of grade school, the results were less satisfactory in the college of Celana, so that he was occasionally scolded by his parents. It is probable that the fact of being away from home, the exhausting daily trip, and the different locale had an adverse effect on the boy.

Meanwhile, he began to cherish hopes of becoming a priest. His parents approved of the idea and arranged to send him to the diocesan seminary of Bergamo at the age of eleven years. But a serious difficulty developed: he had to be provided with suitable clothing and there was very little money. His mother, at the suggestion of the parish priest,

Don Rebuzzini, finally decided to go the rounds of the relatives, but when evening came, all she returned with was two lire (about 1,000 lire or two dollars in today's money).

But young Angelo Roncalli left for the city. A large part of his boarding expenses were taken care of by a generous benefactor, Msgr. Morlani.

AT THE SEMINARY

The year 1892 marked a turning point in the life of the future pope. It was then that Angelo entered the seminary and for eight years, until 1900, pursued the usual gymnasium and lyceum courses. It was at this period that he gradually gave evidence of possessing undoubted gifts of intelligence and character.

At first, in fact, the young boy found that he had to overcome many difficulties connected with his new environment and with adapting himself to the heavy load of study which was new to him. But after the first few years a change took place in him, revealing his unusual talents, his profound humility, above all the will to succeed, confidence in himself, and a proper sense of pride.

At the same time he gave evidence in many ways of his goodness of soul. He frequently would help his less capable fellow-students with their work and sometimes shared with them the little money he received from home to supplement his meager seminary fare.

On June 28, 1895, he received tonsure. At 16

he was named prefect of the dormitory, and the following year, in 1898, he received major orders.

In 1900 he was graduated with honors from the lyceum and in view of his intellectual and devotional attainments evidenced during eight years of study, he was chosen by his bishop to attend the Collegio Ceresoli [2] in Rome, so that he could pursue his courses in higher theology at the Roman seminary.

A STUDENT AT ROME

"Ever since I was born I have had no thought of becoming anything else than a priest," said Patriarch Roncalli in a speech at San Marco.

Now he was at Rome, a student in the famous old seminary, where he had as spiritual director Father Francesco Pitocchi, a priest of rare ability and great piety, who died in the odor of sanctity in 1922.

Some of his former fellow-students, likewise from Bergamo and now priests in the diocese, remember that even in his first years it was predicted that their colleague would rise high in the hierarchy of the Church. The strong impression made by his personality, his intelligence, and his goodness guaranteed this.

After the prescribed four years of study, Angelo Roncalli obtained the laureate (doctorate) in theology.

[2] A college with scholarships for young Bergamask students who have been chosen to complete their higher studies in theology and law at Rome.

Bergamo and Rome

Two future supreme pontiffs were present in the halls of the Roman seminary in those days. The theme of the written examination in theology, perhaps the most difficult of all which the young clerics had to pass, was set by a young, tall, slender, straight-as-a-ramrod priest dressed in tailored black cassock, Eugenio Pacelli, the future Pius XII. And among those who were being examined was the future John XXIII.

HIS FIRST YEARS AS A PRIEST

At twenty-three Angelo Giuseppe Roncalli was ordained priest by Bishop Ceppetelli, Vicar of Rome, in the church of Santa Maria in Monte Santo in the Piazza del Popolo. This date, August 10, 1904, marked the beginning of a mission the importance and goal of which were clear even then to the new young priest.

"A priest is supposed to comfort and enlighten souls, and he is able to fulfill this mission because he himself feels the weight of human frailty. His task is above all to dispense grace, to administer the sacraments." Again, speaking of himself, he said, ". . . the humble son of the people was raised to a wonderful office which enables him to benefit the people by a daily offering of gifts and sacrifices to the Lord, to a ministry of propitiation for sins and sinners, to a role of constant dedication."

He naturally wished to celebrate his first Mass at the tomb of St. Peter. On that very day, August 11, 1904, the new priest had the great joy to be ad-

mitted to the presence of Pope St. Pius X. Forty-
nine years later the Patriarch of Venice thus recalled this encounter: "I had the joy and good
fortune to see Saint Pius X the very day I celebrated Mass for the first time at the tomb of St.
Peter on August 11, 1904. When the Holy Father
appeared, someone who was accompanying me said,
'Holy Father, this is a young priest from Bergamo
who has just said his first Mass this morning.' Pius
X placed both his hands on my head and said:
'Bravo, I bless you and encourage you to be an
honor to your high calling, and I hope that your
priesthood will be a consolation to the Church of
God.'" Shortly afterward he returned to Bergamo
and celebrated his first Mass in his native homeland, on August 15, the Feast of the Assumption.
The first person whom he met on his return to
Sotto il Monte on that occasion was an old friend
of the family, a certain Dr. Cesare Mingozzi. The
latter congratulated him warmly on his ordination
to the priesthood and, embracing him affection-
ately, told him, "Bravo Don Angelo, some day you
will be pope." Ever since then Don Roncalli used
to love to remind his friends of this "prophecy,"
smiling as he did so at the thought, as he did at so
much else that was customarily said on these occasions.

Again we find him at Rome for the consecration of certain bishops on January 20, 1905, among
whom was Giovanni Radini-Tedeschi, destined by
that discerner of men and pastor of souls, St. Pius
X, to govern the diocese of Bergamo. Of a noble

family from Piacenza, a follower of the political line of Cardinal Rampolla and a favorite of Leo XIII, a man of rare intelligence, character, and devotion, Bishop Radini-Tedeschi was one of the first and most important promoters of Catholic social action in Italy, which spread throughout his diocese. Having to choose a secretary, the new bishop thought of picking one of the two young priests who had assisted at the Mass celebrated by Pius X in the Sistine Chapel on the occasion of his consecration.

"When, shortly before leaving for Bergamo to take formal possession of his new see, Bishop Radini-Tedeschi asked the rector of the Roman seminary to indicate which one of the Bergamask priests he should choose as secretary, he chose Don Angelo Roncalli and me," remembers Msgr. Guglielmo Carozzi, fellow-student of the pope and the one who served with him at the Mass. "But the rector suggested Roncalli as the more suitable because he was 'more Romanized.' "

Thus it was that Bishop Radini-Tedeschi chose Don Angelo Roncalli. Two men of such completely different social background, temperament, and habits found themselves obliged to live together thereafter, on a daily and even hourly basis. The spirit of sincere, cordial collaboration of the one, with his air of the enlightened *grand seigneur,* was matched by the admiring obedience, fidelity, and dynamic energy of the other.

For nine years, from 1905 to 1914 (when Bishop Radini-Tedeschi died), the secretary stood by his

15

side, gaining an immeasurable wealth of practical experience, and above all deep, living spirituality. Bishop Radini-Tedeschi was the star of Don Roncalli's priesthood. A trace of their closeness and life shared together would remain with the young priest and the image of the bishop of Bergamo would reappear to him in a thousand circumstances, conversations, memories, warnings, and prayers. It would always be a living reality to the mind of Angelo Roncalli, who regarded him as his venerable teacher and beloved father.

These nine years were ones of active preparation for the young priest for the future, higher responsibilities which would later be entrusted to him. The bishop of Bergamo was termed an inflexible "social bishop" at a difficult time when it seemed that the solution to certain perplexing problems must remain exclusively in the hands of political parties completely outside the orbit of the Church. The bishop's mission was arduous and delicate, but it was accomplished with great devotion, aided by his profound learning and great charity, an admirable example of selfless devotion to duty for his young secretary.

As a testimony of his gratitude for this example of devotion which had such an influence on him, the former secretary dedicated the large volume which he wrote in 1916 to the memory of "his" bishop.

Numerous incidents in the life of Radini-Tedeschi are recalled by the present pope. Particularly moving were the last few hours of this illustrious prelate. Before the bishop's death, thinking that he was unconscious, Don Angelo Roncalli began to recite the prayers for the dying, but the bishop said to him in a weak voice, "Courage, courage, Don Angelo; it is all right, please go on, I understand all, you know. . . ." Every year during his summer vacation at Sotto il Monte, Roncalli used to celebrate a Mass at the tomb of Bishop Radini-Tedeschi for the repose of his soul.

As a precious heirloom, he has preserved the cassock which the bishop of Bergamo wore during that memorable consecration of January 20, 1905, and it is said that he used it during the conclave which ended in his own election.

Among the many tasks which fell to the lot of the young secretary was that of making frequent trips, from which Don Angelo Roncalli always sought to derive profit, through study and research, especially in the Ambrosian Library in Milan. This, however, did not prevent the young cleric from devoting himself to teaching. It was in this period that he was appointed *docent* in ecclesiastical history and apologetics at the lyceum of the seminary at Bergamo (1906-1912), and later in patrology. He devoted to teaching all his free time when not busy with the work of the diocesan curia.

"His lectures were always followed with great interest both for their content and the personality of the professor," according to Msgr. Pietro Carrara, the present vicar-general of the diocese of Bergamo and a student during the time of Don Roncalli. The present spiritual director of the same seminary, Father Angiolini, also remembers, "He was my professor in apologetics at the lyceum for three years, from 1909 to 1912. I shall never forget the gentle, persuasive manner of his teaching. He was always very pleasing and interesting to listen to." Professor Baronchelli, who was also a teacher in the same school, remembers his professor of apologetics with fondness, particularly the motto which has remained inscribed on his memory: "Always be prepared to answer anyone who demands a reason for your faith. . . ."

His preparation during these years (1906-1915) was completed and refined, as it were, by trips to France, Palestine, and Spain with Bishop Radini-Tedeschi and also for the Association for Pilgrimages. Roncalli derived great profit from these trips. They were for him—acute observer of men and scenes as he then was—an eye-opener on the world, beyond the limited compass of merely diocesan problems.

In November, 1904, he joined the diocesan Congregation of Priests of the Sacred Heart. He made his first vows as a member on November 4, 1912, and on January 6, 1917, took his perpetual vows.

IN THE ARMY

Europe had been at war since September 3, 1914, when Italy entered the conflict in May, 1915.

Don Angelo Roncalli had already seen brief regular military service in 1901 with the 73rd In-

Birthplace of John XXIII at Sotto il Monte
(Bergamo).

Giordani photo.

Sotto il Monte. The small villa in which John XXIII used to spend his summer vacations.

Giordani photo.

Sergeant Roncalli of the Medical Corps with
other priests mobilized during the First World
War (standing, second from left).

Giordani photo.

Angelo Roncalli as a domestic prelate of His
Holiness, Pope Benedict XV (1921), during
his stay in Rome before being appointed
apostolic visitator to Bulgaria (1925).

Athens. The apostolic delegate to Greece
surrounded by the Catholic bishops after a
plenary conference (May 11, 1938).

Giordani photo.

Beirut. National Eucharistic Congress of Lebanon, 1939 (Cardinal Tisserant in the center; Archbishop Roncalli on the right).

Greece. Apostolic Delegate Roncalli shown
confirming some Italian sailors and marines.

Athens. The Apostolic Delegate Roncalli with members of the Focolari della Divina Providenza (Centers of Divine Providence), the outstanding organization which, guided by him, played an important role in relieving the hardship brought on by the famine of 1942.

Paris. Presentation of New Year's Greetings
as dean of the diplomatic corps to the head
of the provisional French government, General Charles de Gaulle (January 1, 1945).

Giordani photo.

John XXIII in conversation with former-Premier Édouard Herriot.

Nuncio Roncalli in France with his brothers
Giovanni, Saverio, Alfredo and Giuseppe
(1952).

Paris. During a ceremony at the Elysée Palace, with President of the Republic Vincent
Auriol and Foreign Minister Georges Bidault
(center).

Conferring of the cardinal's biretta on Nuncio Roncalli by President of the Republic Vincent Auriol (January, 1953).

Rome. Cardinal Roncalli taking possession
of his titular church of Saint Prisca on the
Aventine (1953).

Giordani photo.

Venice. Solemn entrance of the new patriarch
(March 15, 1953). The procession on the
Grand Canal on the way to the basilica of
San Marco.

Venice. The cardinal patriarch and Archbishop (now Cardinal) Montini of Milan during a ceremony at the Ducal Palace.

fantry Regiment, stationed at the Caserma Umberto I at Bergamo, 8th Company, 4th Platoon.[3]
He was discharged with the rank of sergeant after six months, on September 14, 1901. One of his comrades in arms of those days, a certain Giuseppe Manenti, remembers, "One day Roncalli, who was my instructor, threw himself down on his cot discouraged. I asked him what the matter was. 'Didn't you see that thirty new recruits have arrived from the south? Well, instead of assigning a few of them to the other instructors (that is, Zonca, Crotti and Giavarini, seminary students like Roncalli), they gave them all to me. They don't know anything; they can't even tell their right hand from their left; they don't know how to read. Goodness knows how poor and destitute they must be at home.' "
At the end of its training, Sgt. Roncalli's platoon was rated as one of the best, and he received a public acknowledgment for his services.

When in 1916 a general agreement was reached with regard to the status of priests whereby most of them were enlisted as military chaplains with the rank of lieutenant, Don Angelo Roncalli resumed his military career in that capacity with various hospitals in Bergamo. He was also assigned, for a time, to Turin where he was continually

3 His military service was as follows: enrolled as a volunteer for one year in the 73rd Infantry Regiment on November 30, 1901; promoted to corporal on May 31, 1902; discharged with the rank of sergeant on November 30, 1902, on indefinite leave. Recalled through mobilization on May 24, 1915; military chaplain on March 28, 1916; discharged on indefinite leave on February 28, 1919.

busy comforting and aiding the soldiers who were lying wounded in the hospitals of Porta Nuova and La Clementina. Especially during the famous epidemic of "Spanish influenza" his charity was much in evidence. Tirelessly, always cheerful, and with a word of consolation for all, Chaplain Roncalli went wherever he felt that a word from a priest was called for.

In 1919 he was discharged and applied for his accumulated back-pay. The official paymaster, Giuseppe Fumagalli, remembers that, while the clerk was preparing the order for payment, Roncalli gave him his views about military life, observing among other things, "The discipline which makes all men equal in the face of their duty is a great comfort, and brings dignity and comfort to the one who fulfills his duty with zeal, offering the trials and the sacrifices which it entails to the Lord." After the reckoning had been completed, Fumagalli paid him what was owing for four years of service. The total amount did not come to 1,000 lire. Picking up the small sum, Roncalli added: "Well, this is not very much, but it is valuable to me, because I will be able to use it, even to a modest extent, for the Student House which I plan to found in our Bergamo."

The present Holy Father threw some light on his military service and all that it meant to him in a letter written two years ago, while he was patriarch of Venice, to the president of the Association of Chaplains: ". . . I am grateful for everything to the Lord, *qui respexit humilitatem servi sui,* but I especially thank Him for the fact that when I was twenty years old He willed that I should do my military service, and then, during the First World War, renew it as sergeant and chaplain. What a knowledge of the human soul one gains that way! What experience and what grace were given me to dedicate myself, to make sacrifices, to understand life and the apostolate of a priest. . . . If they come to Venice my ex-comrades will always find me ready to welcome them, provided they will let me know beforehand. Their holiday will be my holiday."

In the years following the war he also took an active interest in helping demobilized soldiers adjust to civilian life and in their spiritual welfare, especially in the *"Opera per la Messa del Soldato,"* in the Church of the Holy Spirit.

THE STUDENT HOUSE

He was now also able to devote himself to his project for a "Student House," realized for the first time at the end of the war in 1919, although the basis for the work had been laid in 1915 when the Palazzo Asperti became the property of the diocese.

Seriously disturbed by the predicament of many students in the public secondary schools who had no clubrooms or boarding house (perhaps he remembered his own experience as a poor young student), Don Roncalli intended to found a house

21

they could call their own, with a study-hall, a dining room, recreation and reading rooms, bedrooms, and a chapel.

Demobilized in March, 1919, he devoted himself with great enthusiasm and considerable organizational skill to the realization of the first Student House, of which he was director from 1921 until he was called to Rome.

The house was set up in a part of the Palazzo Asperti and offered the young students both a friendly, dignified sort of place to stay, and a certain amount of useful spiritual guidance. Many of his former pensioners, now for the most part professional people or government officials in their fifties, have fond memories of Don Roncalli's wise and intelligent management of the house in those days.

This institution, the first of its kind to appear in Italy, was later imitated by other dioceses with undoubted benefit to the spiritual and moral education of young students.

When, in 1921, Don Roncalli was called to Rome, the direction of the Student House was entrusted to another priest. Later the institute declined as a result of the removal of the schools to other parts of the city. The Palazzo Asperti still preserves a certain memorial of its first director, the great friend of hundreds of Bergamask students. The memorial is perhaps one that a priest is not wont to leave behind him, namely a large mirror which stands out at the top of the first flight of stairs in the palace.

Some of the guests of those days recall that one
day Don Angelo noticed that certain students were
going out without combing their hair. Hence he
had a large mirror placed here so that everyone
could see himself before going out. "Remember,"
he used to say to his students, "that it is most important to look neat; unless you do, you will not
get ahead." He saw to it that the motto *"Nosce te
ipsum"* ("Know thyself") appeared in large letters
underneath the mirror.

CALLED TO ROME

When the war was over Don Roncalli resumed
teaching at the seminary and gave a course on civilization at the Popular University. He was also at
that time assistant chaplain to the Union of Catholic Women, and, in this post, promoted the foundation of circles or branches of the Union and that
of Catholic Youth in the diocese. One of his talks
at the National Eucharistic Congress of Bergamo
in September, 1920, on "The Eucharist and Our
Lady," received wide acclaim.

At the same time a more exacting duty was assigned to him by Bishop Marelli, namely, that of
being spiritual director of the diocesan seminary,
a post he filled from 1919-1921. As a matter of fact,
when it came time to reopen the seminary at the
end of the war, certain questions were raised concerning the material, and above all the spiritual,
preparedness of many of the young men who were
then emerging from a Red-tainted atmosphere

hardly conducive to the spirit of life which young men who intend to become priests must have. The bishop was therefore particularly eager to entrust the spiritual direction of the new students to a priest of proven ability, wide experience, and sound doctrine. The choice could hardly have fallen on anyone more suitable than Don Roncalli, and turned out to be most fortunate as the encouraging results, achieved in a short space of time, gave evidence. The clergy of Bergamo emerged strengthened from this period of trial, thanks to the strong personality, ability, and tact of the spiritual director, and were able to make a brilliant contribution toward overcoming the difficulties of the hour.

He always had fond memories of "his" seminary, even when he was elevated to higher ranks in the hierarchy. The rector, Msgr. Luigi Sonzogni, recalls that Roncalli made a gift of the 500 volumes of Migne's *Patrologia Latina* and *Graeca,* and has made many private visits to the institution.

In the course of time the reputation of the young priest reached the Vatican. His remarkable abilities as an organizer induced Pope Benedict XV to summon him to Rome in 1921, at a time when the subsidiary associations dependent on the Sacred Congregation for Propagating the Faith, which until then had had their headquarters in France, were being reorganized.

To Msgr. Roncalli was entrusted the presidency of the National Committee for Italy of the

"Opera per la Propagazione della Fede" (Associa-tion for the Propagation of the Faith).

Futher work was placed on his shoulders by Pope Pius XI, who was particularly eager to ex-pand the far-flung work of the missions. Having meanwhile been named honorary canon of Ber-gamo and a domestic prelate, Msgr. Roncalli now devoted himself to the foundation of various re-gional centers in Italy for the *"Opera per la Propa-gazione della Fede."*

He was later appointed member of the higher international council of the *"opera"* (*Consiglio Superiore Internazionale*) and took an active part in its work, being partly responsible for the fram-ing of its statutes.

During four years of continual work which fre-quently took him outside Italy (during these years he made trips to Lyons, Paris, Brussels, Aix-la-Chapelle, Munich, and other European centers), he promoted the various projects agreed upon by the higher council, laying the basis for an even more promising and rewarding harvest of Cath-olic missions in the future.

This multifarious activity of Msgr. Roncalli in Rome, as during former periods of his life, did not prevent him from pursuing his pastoral charge as a priest, hearing confessions, preaching, con-ducting retreats for persons in all walks of life, tasks which constituted a pleasant apostolic duty for him in the midst of his usual labors.

During these years he also occasionally taught

patristics at the Pontifical Lateran Seminary, of which he has always had fond memories.

The approval which Msgr. Roncalli found in Rome and the esteem in which he was held on all sides were manifested on the occasion of his episcopal consecration in March, 1925. The church of San Carlo al Corso was full of persons from all walks of life for this great event.

The *Osservatore Romano*—always rather conservative in its judgments—wrote on March 26, 1925: "His sound piety, rare intelligence, formidable learning, ardent and effective zeal, his wide harvest of accomplishment as a priest, sensitive Christian manner, fine sense of judgment, perfect sense of balance—these are the things which have won wide esteem, affection and veneration for Bishop Roncalli."

2. Sofia

✠ ✠ ✠

APOSTOLIC VISITATOR AND DELEGATE IN BULGARIA

ANGELO Giuseppe Roncalli arrived in Sofia on the morning of April 25, 1925, from Milan by the Simplon Express, accompanied by his secretary, the Belgian Benedictine Dom Constantin Bosschaerts. He had come to the Bulgarian capital to take possession of his office as apostolic visitator to the Catholic communities of Bulgaria, of both the Latin and Oriental rites.

Pius XI had chosen him for this delicate mission, being himself from Milan and therefore a Lombard like Roncalli, because he admired the intellectual and spiritual gifts as well as the sacerdotal zeal shown by this prelate from Bergamo, who was now forty-three. He was a member of the Central Committee for the Holy Year of 1925 in Rome, when news arrived of his appointment as titular archbishop of Areopolis and apostolic visitator of Bulgaria.[1]

[1] Among the representatives of the Holy See abroad those having diplomatic status must be carefully distinguished from

We Have a Pope

On March 19, 1925, the feast day of St. Joseph, his namesake, he was consecrated in Rome in the national church of the Lombards, San Carlo al Corso, by Cardinal Giovanni Tacci, Secretary of the Sacred Congregation for the Oriental Church, which has charge of the territory of Bulgaria.[2] The

---

those who do not have. Nunciatures and internunciatures belong to the first class; apostolic delegations to the second.

Nuncios are accredited to governments, and (generally) are deans of the local diplomatic corps as a mark of honor. It is their function to promote good relations between the Holy See and the states to which they are accredited, as well as to serve as representatives of the Holy Father with the local episcopate.

Internuncios have the same functions, but do not have the rank of ambassadors like *nuncios,* being the equivalent of ministers plenipotentiary.

Apostolic delegates are also permanent representatives of the Holy Father, but lack diplomatic status. In the territory entrusted to them, which generally comprises several ecclesiastical jurisdictions (dioceses, apostolic vicariates, apostolic prefectures), they watch over the condition of the local church, keeping the Holy Father informed on all matters. Hence they are representatives to the local episcopate, but not accredited to governments.

Both nuncios and apostolic delegates are usually invested with the dignity of archbishop.

Archbishop Roncalli was appointed apostolic delegate on September 21, 1931, when the apostolic delegation was erected in Bulgaria, after the grounds for this step had been carefully prepared for him. When he was sent to Sofia in April, 1925, with the designation of apostolic visitator, as a matter of practice he already exercised the functions of apostolic delegate, but on a temporary and extraordinary basis in accordance with the nature of an apostolic visitation. Archbishop Roncalli became a diplomatic representative in the full sense of the term only when he was appointed apostolic nuncio in France.

[2] While representatives of the Holy See having a diplomatic status—that is, nunciatures and internunciatures—depend directly on the Secretariat of State, apostolic delegations report variously to the Sacred Congregation for the Oriental Church, the Sacred

co-consecrators were the Vicar-General of Rome, Bishop Palica, and the Secretary of the Sacred Congregation for the Propagation of the Faith, Bishop Francesco Marchetti Selvaggiani, later Cardinal.

His first pontifical Mass was celebrated the following day at the tomb of St. Peter, as a re-affirmation of his fidelity to the Apostolic See.

The mission entrusted to Archbishop Roncalli was particularly delicate in view of the conditions and atmosphere in which the Catholics of the Latin rite were living in Bulgaria, and the tribulations through which those of the Oriental rite had gone in the last fifty years. The great mass of the Bulgarian people belong to the Orthodox confession which is recognized by the government—or was—as a "state religion," while the presence of other confessions is merely tolerated.

At the time when he arrived in Sofia as apostolic visitor, the territory of Bulgaria was divided into two ecclesiastical districts so far as the Latin clergy were concerned. In the north was the diocese of Nikopol in charge of a bishop who was a member of the Passionist Fathers, and whose residence was at Ruse. In the south the faithful of the Latin rite depended upon the apostolic vicariate of Sofia and Plovdiv, then in charge of a bishop who belonged to the Capuchin Fathers, with his residence in Sofia.

Congregations of the Consistory, or for the Propagation of the Faith, depending upon the nature of the countries in which the representatives exercise their functions, as seen from the viewpoint of the relations of Catholics with non-Catholics.

We Have a Pope

In the vicariate of Sofia there were about 22,-000 Catholics, for the most part scattered here and there with numerous churches, chapels and houses of religious orders. The clergy comprised twenty secular and forty-eight religious priests, and there were 132 Sisters, some of them teachers, and others attached to hospitals and orphanages in Sofia, Plovdiv, Burgas, Yambol, etc. Catholics had several dozen primary schools, besides eight gymnasiums with several thousand pupils.

In the diocese of Nikopol there were sixteen churches with a population of about 18,000 faithful. The number of Catholic schools was eighteen with about 2,000 pupils, in addition to two lower gymnasiums and two higher ones with a total of 1,200 pupils.

Aside from Latin-rite Catholics, there were also some 4,000 Catholics of the Byzantine rite living in Bulgaria. For their benefit the Holy See had erected an apostolic administration in 1923, on which depended nine churches, eight chapels, five primary schools subsidized by the state, and a number of private schools, with ten lay teachers and twenty-seven religious, both male and female. The Assumptionists, Resurrectionists, and Conventual Franciscans of the Oriental rite assisted the secular clergy of the Oriental rite in the pastoral care of these faithful who were scattered everywhere throughout the territory of Bulgaria.[3]

[3] Today, after thirteen years of communist rule, only a few dozen of the religious priests who were exercising their ministry in Advent, 1944, remain free. Of the three bishops, one died in a

Sofia

It would be wrong to attempt to judge the importance of the mission entrusted to Archbishop Roncalli on the basis of the above figures and the minority status of Catholics in Bulgaria (45,000 Catholics among some 6,000,000 inhabitants, of which fully 85% belonged to the Orthodox confession).

As apostolic visitator, and later as apostolic delegate, he represented in Bulgaria the Holy See and the prestige which it enjoys in the world at large. Both these factors were obviously of far greater weight than the relatively small number of Catholics ever could be in the life of the country. Hence, although he was not invested with diplomatic status, Archbishop Roncalli was able to have, at a time critical for the royal house and the country, numerous contacts with the sovereign and officials of the government in which his gifts as a shrewd and capable diplomat came into play.

At the same time he fulfilled the duties entrusted to him by the Holy See of assisting and reanimating the Catholic communities of the country, especially those of the Oriental rite, which had grown following the arrival of numerous refugees from Macedonia and Thrace as a result of World War I; of introducing modern forms of the apostolate, and especially Catholic Action; of revitalizing the Catholic schools; of settling questions relating

---

communist prison, another, who is now insane, is kept in an asylum for the criminally insane, while the third—the Exarch for Catholics of the Oriental rite—seems to be free but is impeded in the exercise of his ministry.

31

to mixed marriages between Catholics and Orthodox; of cementing unity between Catholics of both rites by means of his authority as representative of the head of the Church.

The day after his arrival he assisted at a sung Mass of the Byzantine rite in the Byzantine Catholic church in Sofia. At the end of the service he had his first contact with the many priests and faithful who had come to pay homage to the representative of the pontiff.

Four days later Archbishop Roncalli paid a visit to King Boris with whom he had a long talk. He then went to pay his respects to the Minister of Foreign Affairs and other high dignitaries.

Then he took in hand the business of the apostolic visitation, making it his special care to study the ways in which he could improve the training of the clergy and set on foot a plan—later accomplished, thanks to his efforts—for establishing a seminary. He also took note of the needs of the Catholic schools and coordinated and directed the efforts of the three Bulgarian bishops to ward off the threatened nationalization of Catholic educational institutions by a hostile government.

In order to assure the success of his mission, he sought to learn everything he could about the history, traditions, and customs of the country. He applied himself to the rather formidable task of learning the Cyrillic alphabet and Slavic accentuation and became fluent enough to read with ease —a tribute to his Bergamask tenacity. He frequently advised foreign priests that they should learn Bulgarian and set an example himself on many occasions. In 1927, for instance, he delivered part of his Christmas sermon in Bulgarian.

During his stay in Bulgaria, a severe economic crisis brought great hardship to many of the people. With the same charity he had manifested during the war and which would be one of the outstanding features of his later stay in Athens, the apostolic delegate undertook to do all he could to relieve the suffering of the Bulgarian people.

Every day large numbers of the poor and starving came to the doors of his residence in Sofia, begging alms and food. All who came were helped, with no regard for their social position or religious affiliation.

When certain areas of the country were hard hit by earthquake in December, 1928, he sought and received assistance from the Holy See and undertook its distribution personally.

According to a remark once made by him, contact with the Slavs—a people who are sometimes difficult for Westerners to deal with—stimulated in him a sense of gentleness and patience.

His knowledge of the language and his gentle and charitable manner bore fruit in helping to strengthen the spiritual side of the Church in the midst of an almost entirely Orthodox society, which was frequently so prejudiced toward everything Catholic.

Three months after his arrival in Bulgaria, there appeared in Sofia's French-language daily newspaper, *La Bulgarie,* a description of the visitation he had made, characterized by a sense of appreciation for what he had done. It was the same kind of sympathy he would inspire in his collaborators, journalists, priests, bishops, diplomats and government officials in Greece, Turkey, Paris and Venice:

We entered the forecourt of the [Byzantine Rite] church of Sofia, where Archbishop Roncalli lives in a white house. A Bulgarian priest led us into a simple but elegant room. Soon the door of the Archbishop's study opened and we saw His Excellency rise, leaving his desk laden with books. On a small bookstand are several Fathers of the Church, as well as several volumes of the great Italian authors, Dante, Petrarch, Manzoni, etc. Archbishop Roncalli is still relatively young, his face is striking for its energy, sincerity, and gentleness. He received us with warmth and simplicity. . . . His face lit up with intense joy when we spoke to him about our country, our simple but kindly peasants, of whom he has heard so much and with whom he is already in touch. . . .

HIS LOVE FOR THE EASTERN CHURCH

The nearly ten years which Archbishop Roncalli spent in Bulgaria gave him unique opportunity to know that Eastern Church at first hand, which he had already learned so much about in his studies.

He came to know it and love it.

Sofia

He never tired repeating that it was possible to be at the same time both good Orientals and good Catholics, because the Church of Rome respects— a respect which he made the basis of his mission there—the institutions, customs, rites and language of the Catholic faithful of Oriental rites.

It was extremely painful for him when he learned at the end of World War II, while apostolic delegate in Istanbul and nuncio in Paris, of the devastation wrought by the communist regimes among Bulgarian Catholics of the Oriental rite and among all the Catholic communities in the East who happened to find themselves under Marxist governments at the end of the war.

One of the aims of his apostolic visitation was to prepare for the nomination of a bishop for the Oriental Catholics. In 1926 he succeeded in having the provisional apostolic administration for Catholics of Byzantine rite resident in Bulgaria replaced by a permanent apostolic exarchate, for which he proposed a suitable candidate to Rome.

As evidence of his love for the Eastern Church we may cite the words which he dedicated to it in the message which he delivered to the world the day after his election as supreme pontiff:

And just as We embrace the Western Church, so with equal paternal affection We also embrace the Eastern Church; and We open Our heart and Our arms to all those who are separated from this Apostolic See where Peter himself lives in his successors until the consummation of the world and fulfills the command

35

given him by Christ to bind and loose everything on earth and feed the sheep of the Lord.

We desire ardently their return to the house of the common Father and therefore repeat the words of the Divine Saviour: "Holy Father, preserve in Thy name those whom Thou hast entrusted to Me that they may be one even as We are one!" In this way "there will be one sheepfold and one shepherd."

Let all therefore come, We beseech them, and shortly bring about this return with the inspiration and aid of grace. They will not be entering a strange house, but their own, the same which was formerly made illustrious by the glorious doctrine of their ancestors and made precious by their virtues.

In September, 1957, when delivering the opening discourse at the Eastern Christianity Week at Palermo, he concluded his speech with the question: "Is the responsibility all on the side of our separated brethren? It is partly theirs, but largely also ours, since it belongs to us to soothe the grief of those who suffer in schism, by deed, word, the example of our humility, and charity—above all by those virtues which triumph over every obstacle."

John XXIII retains with him on the papal throne this first-hand knowledge of the Eastern world and its problems. He is the only pope for many centuries who has lived for a long time in the midst of Oriental Christians and knows the various churches of Oriental rite personally.

That can only be a good sign for the future of Christendom under the aegis of the one sheepfold of Christ.

Sofia

THE DIPLOMAT

An historical event provided the occasion for Apostolic Delegate Roncalli to emerge from the habitual reserve with which he was carrying on his purely ecclesiastical mission among the Catholics of Bulgaria. On this occasion he carried out the instructions received from Rome with fine diplomatic tact, as well as with appropriate vigor. The episode then had a considerable echo in the international press, in view of the high rank of the persons involved. It is important, however, first to recall the historical setting.

On July 7, 1887, under the influence of President of the Council Stamboulof, an open enemy of the Russians, the Bulgarian National Assembly had chosen as its second ruler the German Prince Ferdinand of Saxe-Coburg-Gotha, who was a Catholic.

The new sovereign could continue in this faith according to the Bulgarian constitution, but he was obliged to see that the heir apparent was baptized in the Orthodox Church.

After obtaining an assurance that this provision of the constitution would be changed, King Ferdinand contracted a marriage on April 20, 1893, with the Catholic Princess Maria Luisa of Parma. Premier Stamboulof succeeded in modifying the constitution so that it was not necessary for the crown prince to belong to the Orthodox faith. But the king, in the interests of stabilizing the dynasty, wished to have good relations with Russia. Hence it was that, on February 2, 1896, the crown prince Boris was baptized in the Orthodox cathedral of Sofia. Leo XIII had not failed to point out to the king that he was embarking on a path that would lead to eventual excommunication.

The queen died in 1899 from the grief which the step caused her. In 1908 King Ferdinand was married again, this time to Princess Eleanor of Reuss, a Protestant.

On July 8, 1908, the Bulgarian constitution was again changed. Article 38 now read: "The King of Bulgaria cannot belong to any other religion than the Orthodox faith." When Boris ascended the throne on October 3, 1918, the royal household conformed to this provision. Princess Eudossia, however, sister of King Boris, had been baptized in the Catholic faith and remained a Catholic. She would be quite close to Archbishop Roncalli during the ten years he sojourned in Bulgaria.

On October 5, 1930, the engagement was announced between King Boris and Princess Giovanna, daughter of the King of Italy. A few days later, an official communiqué appeared in the *Osservatore Romano*, noting that Princess Giovanna, in a letter signed by her and King Boris, had requested Pope Pius XI for permission to contract a mixed marriage, solemnly promising to give the necessary guarantees (recognizing the validity of the marriage contract and unlawfulness of any repetition of the nuptial ceremony; maintenance of the Catholic faith on the part of the

Catholic; education of the children in the Catholic faith). The princess requested, at the same time, permission for the nuptial ceremony to take place in the basilica of St. Francis at Assisi.

The pope granted both requests. The nuptial blessing was imparted to the couple at Assisi on October 25, 1930. Notwithstanding their position as reigning sovereigns, the Church limited the ceremony of the rite to that provided for mixed marriages.

Suddenly, after their arrival back in Sofia, the sovereigns went through another ceremony in the Orthodox cathedral of Sofia. Since in Bulgaria the functions of state officials are also exercised by Orthodox priests, it was said that the spouses had to go to an Orthodox church. The question therefore arose whether a proper religious marriage ceremony had taken place or simply a civil formality accompanied by a blessing. The government of Bulgaria and the Holy Synod held that it was a question of an Orthodox religious service and such was also the opinion of the people, judging from official statements and the Bulgarian press. It was said that the Queen Giovanna was weeping when she returned from the Orthodox ceremony.

The Holy See was obliged to put on the lamentable affair the interpretation which the Bulgarian government gave to the incident, and Pope Pius XI in his consistorial allocution of December 24, 1930, had these grave words to say:

. . . concerning such conditions and guarantees We
have treated, not with the political personalities of a
country or any government, but with the royal con-
tractants themselves, who assumed formal and written
responsibility for them explicitly mentioning the relative canons, and expressed in such a way as to inspire
full and absolute confidence (this is clear from their
status as august persons) that they fully intended to
live up to the undertaking agreed to, and, with perfect
loyalty as sovereigns, assumed the obligation of maintaining it.

It was the task of Apostolic Delegate Roncalli
to express to the sovereigns the surprise and dis-
pleasure of Pius XI at their action which, in the
opinion of the Holy See, could not be justified
even by the difficult political condition of the
country.

Since the Bulgarian government replied to the
protest of the apostolic delegate that without prej-
udice to the Catholic marriage of the king, the intention was to conform strictly to the norms of the
constitution, it was necessary to wait and see what
would arise on the occasion of the baptism of the
new heir apparent.

A daughter was born to the royal couple on
January 14, 1933. In great haste, even before the
Queen of Italy had arrived in Sofia, the little
princess was baptized in the Orthodox Church in
the chapel of the royal palace. She was named
Maria Luisa in memory of the mother of the king.

The constitution provided that only the king
(and consequently, the heir to the throne, but not

other members of the royal family) should belong to the Orthodox faith.

The very day of the baptism, Apostolic Delegate Roncalli requested an audience with the President of the Council Mouchanof, to whom he presented a solemn protest on the part of the Holy See.

On January 18, 1933, the following communication was printed in the *Osservatore Romano:*

Following the baptism administered to the newborn princess by the non-Catholic metropolitan Stephen, the Apostolic Delegate, Archbishop Roncalli, presented in the usual way an energetic protest against the nonfulfillment of the obligations undertaken, in accordance with the sacred canons, by the august parents of the princess before the celebration of their marriage, to obtain from the Holy See the necessary dispensation from the impediment of a mixed marriage.

Archbishop Roncalli also protested to King Boris. To these moves of the apostolic delegate the Bulgarian government gave no reply except to state that the baptism had taken place as a result of a decision taken by the head of state and the government "according to the constitution" and in conformity with the will of the Bulgarian people. Prince Simeon, the present king-in-exile and the couple's second child, was also baptized according to the Orthodox rite.

Assisted and comforted in her spiritual sufferings by the apostolic delegate, Queen Giovanna, like a "stranger" in Bulgaria, had much to suffer for various reasons, and always will regard him with the greatest affection and filial devotion. She was present at his coronation as pope in St. Peter's.

Only future historians, who can consult the archives of the Holy See, will be able to give a complete description of the part played by Archbishop Roncalli in this painful incident.

3. Istanbul and Athens

✠ ✠ ✠

APOSTOLIC DELEGATE IN TURKEY

THE apostolic delegate in Turkey and Greece, Msgr. Margotti, was appointed Archbishop of Gorizia and Gradisca on July 24, 1934. To succeed him in both posts Pius XI called on the apostolic delegate in Bulgaria, whose profound knowledge of the Eastern world, gained in the course of his tour of duty there, he greatly appreciated, as well as his rare gifts of tact and prudence displayed in a difficult mission.

Archbishop Roncalli was appointed apostolic delegate and arrived in Greece on November 19 of that year and a few days later was named apostolic delegate to Turkey and administrator of the apostolic vicariate of Constantinople (Istanbul). Having resigned his titular see of Areopolis, the new delegate became titular Archbishop of Mesembria, the see which had been held by his predecessor Msgr. Margotti and which he would continue to hold until his elevation to the cardinalate.

Although the apostolic delegation in Turkey

43

had lost much of its importance since its foundation in 1868 when its jurisdiction extended over
the vast expanse of the Ottoman Empire, it re-
tained jurisdiction over so-called "European Turkey" (vicariate apostolic of Constantinople for the
faithful of the Latin rite; apostolic exarchate for
Catholics of the Byzantine rite; archbishopric for
the Catholic Armenians), and over Asiatic Turkey
(with numerous ecclesiastical jurisdictions for the
faithful of the Armenian rite and certain dioceses
of Catholics of the Chaldean, Syrian, and Latin
rites).

At the time when Archbishop Roncalli took
charge, the apostolic vicariate of Constantinople,
which had been erected originally in 1742, comprised forty-nine churches with sixty-five priests
and about 10,000 faithful.

On the apostolic delegation in Greece, erected
in 1834, depended the ecclesiastical districts for
Catholics of the Latin rite on the mainland
(Athens and Thessalonica) and the Greek isles; the
apostolic exarchate of Athens for Catholics of the
Byzantine rite; and an ordinariate for the Armenians.

Only the historian who will be able to consult
the Vatican Archives sometime in the future will
be able to describe the part which Archbishop
Roncalli played in handling the delicate questions
which came to the fore during most of his ten-year
stay as apostolic delegate in Greece and Turkey.
Reference however should be made to the contacts

which took place on neutral Turkish territory during the Second World War, in view of the simultaneous presence there of diplomatic representatives of both sides in the conflict.

The future historian will also be able to study the part which Roncalli had in helping to normalize the relations between the Holy See and Greece, poisoned by misunderstanding with regard to the Catholic Church, especially because of the presence in Greece of faithful of the Oriental rite.

It will also be for him, relying on official documents, to describe the efforts of Roncalli to reach a mutual understanding, a *rapprochement,* and a reunion between the Catholic Church and the Oriental churches separated from Rome under the leadership of the Orthodox patriarch of Constantinople. The study of the Christian East and the causes of the separation from the center of Christendom were, as a matter of fact, one of his most constant preoccupations. The thought which inspired him during the twenty years of his activity in the East as apostolic delegate was the Pauline principle that the Church is neither Latin, Greek, nor Slav, but properly Catholic, that is, universal. (Benedict XV's famous phrase deserves to be recalled in this connection: "The Church of Jesus Christ is neither Latin nor Greek nor Slav, but Catholic . . . all are equal in the eyes of the Apostolic See.")

Leaving to the historian of the future the task of studying the important details of his mission there, we shall confine ourselves to discussing certain general aspects of his activity in Istanbul and Athens.

The new apostolic delegate to Turkey arrived in Istanbul on the Orient-Express, from Sofia, on January 4, 1935. He did not want anyone to meet him at the station except the secretary of the apostolic delegation, Msgr. Angelo Dell'Acqua.[1] It did not appear appropriate, as a matter of fact, to draw attention to the new delegate by means of public demonstrations, since his presence on Turkish soil was merely tolerated by the Turkish government. Moreover, his mission was of a purely ecclesiastical nature scarcely in conformity with the strictly secular spirit of the Turkish state. (It should be borne in mind that the law then in force, among other things, forbade the wearing in public of any dress which signified that one belonged to any religious confession.[2])

Two hours after his arrival the dynamic new apostolic delegate was calling upon the Vali (gov-

[1] After this first meeting with his secretary, Archbishop Roncalli always had the greatest affection and esteem for Msgr. Dell'Acqua. He would again come across him in the Vatican, as successor to Cardinal Montini in the post of Substitute Secretary of State at the time of his elevation to the supreme pontificate.

[2] Modern Turkey purports to be a national, lay state, which has expelled all national minorities from Asia Minor, tolerating them only in Istanbul. The Treaty of Lausanne after World War I no longer offered the minorities any effective guarantee and European states henceforth abandoned their protectorates in the Near East because the maintenance of this right was no longer of any advantage to the protected.

ernor) of the city and the chief of police. Later he received the homage of the chapter and clergy of the cathedral in his residence.

He took formal possession as administrator of the apostolic vicariate and had his first contacts with the faithful entrusted to his pastoral care on January 6, the Feast of Epiphany. On this occasion Archbishop Roncalli delivered an address in which he mentioned themes dear to his heart when later called to even higher responsibilities as a shepherd of souls, first at Venice and then later at Rome as supreme pontiff. The following are a few of the things he said at this time:

At last I am at your service! You were waiting for me; I was told and read that I had already been chosen in your thoughts and hearts even before the Holy Father had entrusted me with the apostolate to be your pastor. It is only in deference to obedience that I have come. Thus it is not you to whom I owe my selection, but it is indeed to you to whom I am grateful for your charity and the honor with which you have greeted me this morning by showing me your filial regard. May you be blessed both now and forever!

During these last few weeks I have had to fight a battle in my heart while I left other brothers and sons who for ten years had been the object of my care and who were always a source of consolation to me—I wish to emphasize this and repeat it to their credit—and of pleasure, and whom I shall never cease to love as long as I live. But now my heart opens like arms that bless and leans toward you who are to form my new spiritual family. How could I not love you, not place

47

myself entirely at your service for the good of your souls? or even make sacrifices for you whenever it shall be necessary? May God grant me the grace to do so!

I wished to greet you on this great Christian Feast of the Epiphany of the Lord, that the inauguration of my pastoral ministry may appear as a gift of our souls together to Jesus, of a renewal of our consecration to Him. . . .

Oh my brethren and sons! Can one find any better way in which to express the duties of a shepherd of souls such as you expect me to be? You know very well, and all the world knows well, that I have not been sent here to conduct politics or look after material interests: *my functions are absolutely and exclusively religious. And it is on these grounds that I wish to, and must, remain at all costs.* Your souls are what I seek, your advancement in the spiritual life, which leads inevitably to further progress in the temporal and social fields. It is by the Lord's charity that we avoid evil which offends Him and His gospel, and it is also a living flame illuminating and stimulating us to noble actions which do honor to the citizen in all the walks of private and public life. . . .

I wish to imitate—I would even like to rival if possible—the brilliant example set by my predecessors who were fond not only of honoring with their presence but edifying with their devotion the sacred rites which so frequently and with such care are wont to be held in this basilica-cathedral or in the principal churches of the city. And it is in this light of mystical elevation round the sacred altars, in the midst of the incense-laden air, that it would please me to see again and to evoke the memorable image of the last two apostolic delegates whom I had the honor to admire here, where they often invited me on the occasion of solemn religious feasts, and who seemed to be initiating me, as it were, to be their successor. . . . Each had a spirit which was proper to him, but every spirit praises the Lord: *omnis spiritus laudet Dominum.* I regard myself as quite small by comparison with them, splendors of the Catholic episcopate, and I tremble to think that I am succeeding them. But I hope that I can imitate their virtues and, joining their ranks, do honor to the tradition of each, having been called to work in the same part of the vineyard first tilled by them and to apply the valuable and wise measures which they have proposed with greater or less solemnity. . . .

My brethren, my sons! you who feel the weight of grief, you whose shoulders bend under the load of human misery, you whose soul is sorry with the uncertain vision of the future, let me inspire you with courage, let me comfort you from the first moment of my meeting with you.

It is a rule of life that the accomplishment of every duty involves a sacrifice. Do not think that the children of this world who do not profess any consoling faith do not suffer in accomplishing their tasks. They may also suffer more than we do, how much more! But we bear our sufferings with equanimity, with dignity, and they become something light and easy.

My brethren and sons! behold me before the altar to offer to Jesus my myrrh, my sacrifice. By agreeing to come here, as I have told you, I have only done my duty. Your warmhearted filial greeting, the great esteem which I have had for years and still have for the clergy and Catholic people of Istanbul, make this obedience dear to me. But it does not cease for that reason to be a sacrifice. . . .

We Have a Pope

The new delegate and administrator of the apostolic vicariate at once made a good impression on all because of his piety and simplicity. At the academy held in his honor, the afternoon of the same day, he gave the Catholics a motto for their action: *Frangar non flectar.*

Shortly after this he delivered another sermon in a local church. The Italian ambassador to Turkey, Carlo Galli, was also present. The ambassador would confess twenty years later to a friend that such had been the warmth and fervor of the delegate's words that he, for one, was moved to tears and felt a surge of religious feeling within him.

Ambassador Galli also tells of having invited Archbishop Roncalli to Ankara when the new chapel of the Italian embassy was completed. The following day he also invited the secretary general of the Turkish Ministry of Foreign Affairs, Numan Menemengioglu, for luncheon.[3] At the end of the intimate gathering Roncalli and Menemengioglu had become fast friends, each having recognized in the other the gifts of intelligence, frankness based upon a feeling of mutual trust, utter loyalty to principles, and mutual esteem for each other. They later found themselves together at

[3] The Turkish daily *Aksam* wrote on Oct. 29, 1958: "He [Archbishop Roncalli] won the friendship of numerous persons both in political and private circles . . . one of his greatest friends was the late Numan Menemengioglu. . . . Roncalli had expressed great admiration for Atatürk, and as a friend of the Turks was the one who was the first to order prayers recited in Turkish in the churches of the city."

Paris, the one as apostolic nuncio, the other as ambassador of Turkey. Both then helped to create an atmosphere of understanding and cordiality among the diplomatic corps, despite the difficulties of the immediate postwar period.

The mission entrusted to the new apostolic delegate in Turkey was particularly arduous, as it had been for his predecessors. In addition to the difficulties connected with the minority status (the small number of Catholics in the midst of a large majority of Moslem population; atavistic hostility to the name of "Christian," bound up with humiliating memories for the Ottoman Empire), there were those which stemmed from the lay spirit of the new state founded by Atatürk. The government of Ankara officially "ignored" the existence of the mission entrusted by the Holy See to the apostolic delegate among local Catholics. It only granted it *de facto* recognition, purely out of regard for the personal status of the individual concerned—and Archbishop Roncalli would have occasion to thank the Turkish officials for their extreme courtesy—involving certain facilities accorded only to those with diplomatic status. As for himself, the apostolic delegate was merely a foreigner with a permit to stay in Turkey.

It is therefore understandable how, such being the situation, the apostolic delegate made a point, from the very beginning, of emphasizing the purely religious character of his mission, of abstaining from drawing public attention to his person, of giving evidence on every occasion that he

51

was concerned only with purely ecclesiastical
affairs—as was the case—and of avoiding public
contacts with diplomats. He adopted as his motto:
Non multa loquimur sed vivimus.

All this helped win him a measure of respect
on the part of the Turkish authorities and Turkish
people. He labored—as one of his visitors heard
him say—with much spiritual calm and "like an
ant," without wishing any notoriety for himself or
desiring to become an object of discussion.

Moreover, as apostolic delegate, he did everything possible to convince the Turkish state that it
had nothing to fear from its Catholic subjects. So
far as their duties were concerned he made it clear
that the Holy See and Catholics had no misgivings
with regard to the new Kemalist constitution,
apart from reservations which they were bound to
express with regard to its secularist spirit.

Recognizing moreover in Atatürk a remarkable personality and the advantages to be derived
from his measures for the welfare of the Turkish
people, he saw to it that when the founder of the
new Turkish state died (1938), the Catholics of
Istanbul took part, in a suitable way, in the national mourning.[4] Similar recognition was ac-

4 With regard to Atatürk and Apostolic Delegate Roncalli,
we have a precious testimonial from the ex-ambassador of Turkey, Reckid Saffet Atabinen, published in the daily *Hurriyet* of
Istanbul on November 4, 1958, under the title: "His Holiness
Pope John XXIII as seen by an authentic Turk": ". . . Among
the Moslem and Orthodox circles which we have frequented and
studied for more than half a century, at El Azhar [the famous
university in Cairo] as well as at the Phanar [the seat of the

corded the assumption of the presidency by Ismet Inönü, the right-hand man of Atatürk.

As for himself, Archbishop Roncalli never failed to seize any opportunity to understand the mentality of the Turkish people, study their history, language, traditions, that his attitude might

---

Orthodox Patriarchate of Constantinople] and at Athens, I have never encountered a single ecclesiastical dignitary who could compare with certain high persons with whom I have had contacts at Rome, Paris, and Milan.

"It is sufficient to compare the context of the sermons pronounced by the ulemas at Cairo or Damascus or the Orthodox copyists at Athens or Moscow with the sermons that one sometimes hears in many churches and temples to be aware of the great backwardness of Eastern clergy of all faiths who are glued to a medieval stage, to the hurt of the people whom it is their mission to instruct and lead in the Peace of the Lord.

"These are considerations which I explained to Atatürk more than a quarter of a century ago when it was a question of delivering our compatriots from medieval ignorance and when I told him about my conversations with the eminent apostolic delegate who was at that time Archbishop Angelo Giuseppe Roncalli. The Ghazi much appreciated it, when I informed him of the initiative taken by the representative of the Holy See to have the Sunday sermons in the principal churches of Istanbul and Izmir delivered in Turkish. Archbishop Roncalli himself read in Turkish certain of the prayers at the end of the religious ceremonies. He wished very much to restore, at the cost of Rome, the ancient church of Sts. Sergius and Bacchus, returned to Catholic worship. Had it not been for the ambition of the Egyptians to revive the caliphate under Pan-Arab auspices, which would have interfered in our affairs, the Ghazi, who professed a sincere esteem for Archbishop Roncalli, would have perhaps looked with favor upon the establishment of diplomatic relations with the Vatican, as in the case of France. For a century and a half, he said, Turkey has never had any reason to complain of the loyalty of its Catholic subjects while the Orthodox clergy of Anatolia never ceased conspiring against the vital interests of the country. . . ."

serve as an example to all the Catholics of the
country. He wished that his first pastoral letters
should be written in Turkish and began to have
sermons preached in that language also, which he
made an effort to learn himself.

Knowing that Moslems considered Jesus to be
a great prophet and venerated the mothers of
prophets, and observing that in the church of
Santa Maria in Traperiz (Pera) Moslem women
were wont to go and pray and call upon the
Mother of Jesus, he had placed in this and in other
churches a card with the *Pater Noster* and *Ave
Maria* in Turkish. He thus had the consolation of
seeing even Moslem women reciting the prayers
which are dearest to Catholics. Moreover, Archbishop Roncalli wished that the priests should
recite in Turkish the prayers after Mass, so that all
the faithful could understand what they meant.

Twice a year, he regularly went to Ankara to
visit the Italian parish there. Profiting by this
occasion, he also paid visits to members of the
diplomatic corps.

He neglected nothing which might contribute
to the training of the clergy, so dear to his heart,
and to increase the prestige enjoyed by Catholic
educational institutes in Constantinople, a matter
he considered very important.

In Turkey, as in Bulgaria, the apostolic delegate found ways in which to give expression to
his charity. When a dreadful earthquake shook
Anatolia toward the end of December, 1939, he

obtained a considerable amount of aid from Pius
XII, which he had distributed to the survivors of
the disaster.

DEATH OF HIS FATHER

A journalist from Bergamo tells that once
when he was in Istanbul he visited the apostolic
delegate on August 2, 1935. Before leaving
Bergamo there had been entrusted to him by a
Bergamask friend a letter informing Archbishop
Roncalli about his father's health, since he had
been gravely ill.

As soon as we arrived at the door of his residence,
the servant told us that Archbishop Roncalli was tem-
porarily absent but that he would not be long in re-
turning.

Shortly afterward he came back and the servant
told him that two people from Bergamo were there.
As soon as he came in, he asked us to wait a moment.

After a few moments, the servant took us up to the
first floor to a spacious reception room, where the
archbishop rose to greet us with the utmost courtesy
and affability.

I introduced myself, giving my name, which he
seemed to remember, and then explained to him the
purpose of my visit, that is the desire to pay my respects to him in a country far from our homeland and
the task that had been assigned me in Bergamo of giving him information with regard to the condition of
his father. When I said this, his face seemed to fall
with sadness, which grew as he took note of the con-

tents of the letter. Then he looked up at us and said in a voice full of grief and resignation:

"You have not heard from Bergamo in a couple of days and so could not have known that the truth of today is far different from the good news sent me in this letter. My poor father, who had shown such improvement only a week ago, failed after your departure from Bergamo. I was informed by telegram of his death and I felt the grief of having lost him and not being present at his last moments. But we priests are prepared to be away from our parents and to sacrifice devotion to our family for other more serious duties. Our faith, however, is our greatest comfort, because it gives us the certainty that we shall see our dear ones again in the peace of eternal life.

"Here at Istanbul I have had the consolation of receiving quite a few expressions of condolence from persons in the Italian colony and members of the foreign missions who had learned of my bereavement from the local press."

He then complied with my wish to hear something about his life in Istanbul and his functions in Greece and Turkey.

He said that his life in Istanbul has been quite simple so far as his personal habits were concerned; but there was much activity of a delicate nature with regard to the duties of his office among Catholics and as representative of the Holy See. He did not hesitate to say that he had no means of transportation from one locality to the other, but that he used the public transportation like any one else. His office staff consisted of one secretary, who handled all his correspondence himself both with local Catholics and the authorities, as well as with the Holy See. He gave us to understand that every act of his, whether as a private person or representative of the Holy See, had to be performed with the greatest circumspection, in view of the hostile attitude and difficulties which were placed in the way of a free exercise of the Catholic religion.

Following these frank remarks, I expressed my surprise at his modest and simple habits in view of his high rank and important functions.

I was particularly impressed by his sharp powers of observation, while he was speaking of civic affairs, the manner of life in the country, the condition of the people, their education, charitable programs, and particularly of the profound transformation in the field of ideas resulting from the revolution of the Young Turks, which had overturned the old regime of the Sultan and inaugurated a new form of government of a democratic and progressive character.

In comparing his life in Istanbul with that in Athens, he said that in Turkey his tasks were much more difficult and his work more arduous, while on the other hand in Athens he had had some success and had been able to realize good and conforting results in the exercise of his ministry.

Pope John XXIII will always have a warm memory of his stay in Turkey. The present apostolic delegate at Istanbul, Archbishop Giacomo Testa,[5] after the election of John XXIII, recalled:

[5] Archbishop Testa, also from Bergamo, met the pontiff for the first time in the residence of the bishop of Bergamo, when he was still a young priest. Archbishop Roncalli wanted to take him along as secretary in Bulgaria. Later, Archbishop Testa was auditor with Archbishop Roncalli in Istanbul and chargé d'affaires of the apostolic delegation in Greece. He was later with him in Paris as counselor. He would then be named apostolic delegate to Turkey.

"We met for the last time [Summer, 1958] in Italy, at Bergamo, while passing our vacation there. He asked me to give him a detailed account of new events and changes in Istanbul and told me that, after fourteen years of absence, he earnestly desired to revisit the city. The new pope had a particular predilection for the island of Buyuk Ada where he used to go to spend the summer. One of his greatest delights was to watch the sunsets from a promontory of the island. During our last meeting he said to me in so many words, 'In Turkey I got along fine. I was not simply a diplomat there. I could approach people, interest myself in their troubles and help them. In Turkey I passed some of the most pleasant years of my life.' "

APOSTOLIC DELEGATE IN GREECE

Archbishop Roncalli's actual residence during the years 1935 to 1944 was at Istanbul. He went to Athens from time to time (about twenty times in ten years), not without having to request permission to enter the country each time.

The mission entrusted to him in Greece was also difficult. The apostolic delegate was obliged to proceed with much caution and much uncertainty, in view of the decided reluctance of the Hellenic government to recognize or admit officially a representative of the pope who was to have, even in a strictly religious capacity, any kind of public status. Nevertheless, members of the government, including Prime Minister Metaxas and

King George himself, did not refuse to have private contacts with him.

During the first year after his appointment, the apostolic delegate went to Greece three times and visited the Catholic communities of Athens and some of the islands and made contacts with the episcopate. As a result, he was able to visit all the religious houses of the capital and Piraeus, displaying everywhere that paternal interest and friendly goodness so characteristic of him.

His personal position improved when Greece found itself drawn into World War II.

The principal difficulties for the papal representative came from the presence in Greece of a small group of very active Greek Catholics of the Byzantine rite. In 1923, Bishop George Kalavassy left Turkey because of the difficult political situation and established himself in Greece with a large part of his followers. The appearance of this group of Catholics of Byzantine rite in Greece aroused strong opposition on the part of the national, Orthodox Church. Years of constant bickering and incidents followed and at one point the Catholic Church of the Oriental rite was even legally banned.

Archbishop Roncalli had much to suffer and feared for the fate of Catholicism in Greece when on August 15, 1938, there was published the so-called "Law against Proselytism," which caused difficulty especially for the religious freedom of Catholic citizens. It may be said that every clause of the law was so unjust and oppressive as to make virtually impossible the continued existence of the Catholic Church in Greece, subjecting it to rigid control by the lay authorities.

The Greek episcopate protested, and presented to the head of the government a list of modifications intended to soften the injustices of the law. Though all were not accepted, the law was modified in certain respects (March 22, 1939), partly because of protests which came from outside Greece.[6]

The first draft of the law had defined "proselytism" as an effort to influence, in any manner, the conscience of a member of any religious confession with a view to obtaining a change in his religion. All types of religious propaganda, therefore, were prohibited. The second draft of the law, however, interpreted "proselytism" to mean that propaganda simply which was carried on illicitly, with a promise of material help to those to whom the propaganda was directed, and with the purpose of deceiving or exploiting the ignorance, faith, poverty, or mental weakness of others. Especially punishable was proselytism in schools, centers of learning, or charitable institutions. This type of activity had strong penalties opposed to it.

This incident regarding the "Law against

[6] Certain restrictions governing the publication and sale of Catholic literature were modified, as were regulations insisting on the labeling of Catholic books in such a way as to leave them open to ridicule. The censoring of Catholic books by Orthodox authorities was discontinued. Catholic ecclesiastical officials and clergy were no longer restricted in their travel and entrance of foreign clergy into the country was made easier.

Proselytism" has been recalled to demonstrate the difficulties faced by Archbishop Roncalli in the delicate mission entrusted to him by the Holy See.

It was due in no small measure to his ability that, in ten years' time, a notable improvement took place in the position held by Greek Catholics and an attempt was made to remove the misunderstanding which had so long militated against them. No honest person could henceforth doubt that they were good citizens.

WAR AND FAMINE

During the winter which followed the German-Italian occupation of Greece (1940-1941), a terrible famine broke out among the Greek population. Because of the scarcity of the harvest during the year 1941, the requisitioning of food by the armed forces and, above all, because of the hoarding of supplies by certain speculators, the situation became most acute in the winter of 1942. It is estimated that the number of persons who died from hunger or disease caused by malnutrition amounted to 300,000 after sixteen months of occupation. About 1,000 persons perished each day in Athens alone and as many in Thessalonica at the height of the famine.

The apostolic delegate was ordered by the Holy See to go immediately to Athens from Istanbul and assume coordination of all work of assistance.

Since the state of war had interrupted all means of overland transportation, the apostolic delegate made the trip by car from Istanbul to Sofia and then by air from Sofia to Athens. An enforced stay of ten days at Sofia proved useful for approaching everybody from the king down whom he had known there during his mission.

At Thessalonica Archbishop Roncalli had his first glimpse of crowds of Greek soldiers, wounded and hungry, who sought relief from the Daughters of Charity of St. Vincent de Paul. The Sisters distributed 140 rations every day, thanks to contributions from the American Red Cross. Archbishop Roncalli offered the Sisters a generous donation from the Holy Father.

As soon as he arrived in Athens, Archbishop Roncalli got in touch with the occupation authorities. These visits were not only a matter of protocol, but were necessary in view of the condition of the country. In his contacts with them he outlined his program designed to promote and encourage all types of charitable enterprise, overlooking any considerations of national or religious affiliation. Another program laid before the authorities aimed at providing religious and moral relief in hospitals, prisons, concentration camps and military centers.

In October, 1941, the apostolic delegate also contacted various Greek authorities, among them the President of the Council, General Seraguiglu, Orthodox Metropolitan Damaskinos, the mayor of Athens, and other important civic and ecclesiastical dignitaries.

Istanbul and Athens

The mayor of Athens tendered Archbishop Roncalli a special reception and the event helped set the tone for future relations between the delegate and Greek authorities.

Archbishop Roncalli also set about organizing an information bureau, set up along lines similar to the office in the Vatican. The bureau was meant primarily for prisoners of war and, in July, 1942, for example, the letters and messages received by and sent from the office totaled 40,000.

When he arrived in Athens, Archbishop Roncalli found the *"Monte della Abondanza,"* the charity organization founded by Capuchin Fathers, well established. The organization's purpose was to aid needy families by making food available to them at reasonable prices and, in cases of extreme need, without any cost.

The apostolic delegate encouraged and aided the work of the organization by means of financial support and the formation of a committee to consolidate efforts in raising funds for the *"Monte."*

Another Greek Catholic charitable organization benefited from the interest and encouragement of Archbishop Roncalli. Directed by Bishop George Kalavassy, the apostolic exarch for Byzantine rite Catholics in Greece, the *Estias Pronias* (Centers of Divine Providence) organized soup kitchens which greatly relieved the suffering of thousands of Greeks. The group was also instrumental in establishing hospitals and clinics for babies and small children, the most pitiable vic-

63

tims of the country's famine. Archbishop Roncalli placed Sisters of a Byzantine rite congregation in charge of this work.

Within a short time, sixteen soup kitchens were opened, all sponsored and aided by the apostolic delegate. Much of the food served in the kitchens had been made available through a large gift of the Vatican.

In addition to the distribution of food and child-care services, the *Estias Pronias* also provided medical assistance at a small but well-equipped medical center.

Archbishop Roncalli worked to procure the necessary medicines and other medical supplies for the center and encouraged doctors and pharmacists of Athens to organize themselves into the "Good Samaritan Service," a group which provided medical care for the sick poor.

In addition to these charitable works, Archbishop Roncalli had also his official duties to take care of. Every day, a long stream of people crowded his offices, seeking his help, direction or counsel, and he did not spare himself in his efforts to see them all and do what he could for them.

While at Istanbul, he also took an interest in the lot of the Greek people. On Christmas, 1941, while preaching in the Catholic cathedral in the Turkish capital, he launched an appeal for the charities which were dearest to him. The offerings totaled over 100,000 Italian *lire*.

He also paid numerous visits to English and Greek prisoners of war, in hospitals and in prisons.

His discreet contacts with the occupation authorities facilitated this delicate task. The visit which he paid, with the permission of the German commander, on August 26, 1941, to a camp of English prisoners of war deserves to be remembered, as well as his visits to the military hospitals of Athens, Ellinko, Vula, Arsakian, Sigmalogu. Nor were the visits less fruitful which he paid to the prisons where numerous Greeks were held. Archbishop Roncalli would engage in conversation with them, listening and giving comfort, and quite a few of the prisoners even urged him to thank the Holy Father for all he had done for the Greek people.[7]

After the surrender of Italy in September, 1943, the condition of Greece—which had meanwhile continued to suffer from famine—became steadily worse. Money declined in value and the devalu-

[7] This gratitude for the work of the apostolic delegate in the name of Pius XII is still remembered in Greece. On the day after the election of John XXIII the daily, *Kathimerini,* published an article under the title: "The philanthropic activity of the new pope: the work of Pope John XXIII during the occupation." In the article it was told how, at the entreaty of certain Greek statesmen who had remained in Athens, like Sophoulis, Maximos, Cafandaris, Loghias, Louvaris, and the metropolitan of Athens, Damaskinos, the apostolic delegate had not hesitated to intervene with the Vatican, and even to undertake a trip to Rome, to beg the intervention of Pius XII with the Allies, and particularly England, to obtain a relaxation of the blockade of Greece. Pius XII did intervene and obtained permission for foodstuffs to be sent to Greece to alleviate the suffering. All know and all recognize how effective were the popular canteens organized almost everywhere in Greece by the Red Cross. The Athenians also remember the work of assistance of the "Focolari of Divine Providence" in the name of the Holy Father.

ation created a frightful chaos in the economic and financial situation of the country. A new scarcity of foodstuffs developed and caused prices to soar to incredible heights, compelling the population to live on the little assistance which the Red Cross and the other charitable organizations could provide.

In the chaos which followed the surrender of the Italian troops, the apostolic delegation, under the direction of Archbishop Roncalli in Istanbul, sought to maintain itself apart from and above every manifestation of a tendentious or partisan nature, continuing to labor for the good of all in the spirit of the Gospel and according to the desires of the pope.

By orders of Archbishop Roncalli the delegation staff frequently intervened with the German occupation authorities on behalf of imprisoned priests.

Also assisted were the thousands of Italians whom the events of September, 1943, had thrown into the most wretched condition. Archbishop Roncalli did not cease visiting them, so long as it was possible, in the prisoner of war camps and military hospitals.

The aid granted by the Holy Father to the needy Greeks, through the apostolic delegate, the interventions of the latter on behalf of those unjustly persecuted (Archbishop Roncalli and the Catholic bishops were able on several occasions to plead the case of Greeks with the Italian occupation authorities), the opening of a large Catholic hospital, all these things brought about a decrease in Greek mistrust of the Catholic Church.[8]

It may be said that the mission of Archbishop Roncalli laid the groundwork—slow to mature—of better hopes for the future. The *Osservatore Romano* was able to write, when he was appointed apostolic nuncio to France, on December 23, 1944, in appraisal of his residence in Greece and Turkey: "In these posts, especially during the last few years, amidst *no light difficulties,* he carried out his responsibilities as a faithful executor of the inexhaustible charity of the Holy Father Pius XII."

[8] The Catholic archbishop was able to take part, standing beside the Orthodox archbishop, in the ceremony commemorating the cessation of the war in 1945. This would have been impossible before in a nation where Orthodoxy, besides being a religion, is also something of a political belief.

4. Paris

✠ ✠ ✠

THE DIPLOMATIC REPRESENTATIVE

Toward the middle of December, 1944, a coded dispatch from the Secretariate of State reached the apostolic delegate in Turkey to the effect that His Holiness, Pius XII, had chosen him to be the new apostolic nuncio of the Holy See to France. It is said that in the absence of the secretary of the delegation, the Irish Monsignor Thomas Ryan (in Cairo at the time), Archbishop Roncalli, not very experienced in decoding messages, thought for a while that there had been a mistake. Arriving in Rome, he is reported to have asked the secretary of the Congregation for Extraordinary Ecclesiastical Affairs, Msgr. Tardini,[1] whether there had not perchance been an "error."

The *Osservatore Romano* published on December 23, 1944, an official announcement of the appointment together with a highly flattering account of the new nuncio.

---

[1] Since elevated by John XXIII to the cardinalate and appointed his Secretary of State on November 17, 1958.

69

We Have a Pope

Flying in an American plane by way of Cairo and Rome, Archbishop Roncalli arrived in Paris on December 30, in time to present his credentials to the provisional head of the French government, General Charles de Gaulle, on January 1.

These were particularly difficult times for France and for Europe, indeed for the whole world. The war was still raging in Europe and Asia; in fact, the events we have just related were coincident with General von Rundstedt's offensive in the Ardennes, the famous "Battle of the Bulge"; it was not until January 25 that the Germans were driven back.

France had been profoundly shaken by the war. The nation had experienced defeats and humiliations, the rigors of occupation and the torments of a people divided against itself. Men who had been hailed by some as saviors of their country, like Marshal Pétain or President Laval, now found themselves on trial accused of being traitors to the Fatherland. Minds were confused and upset; moral disintegration was everywhere. France had to be rebuilt from its foundations. But before a fourth republic could come into being, the spirit of the people had to be purged of rancor and suspicion and hatred. War had ceased, or was soon to cease, in France. But spirits remained unpacified.

Perhaps it was precisely with this need for "spiritual" pacification, and the contribution a representative of the Holy See could make toward it, that induced Pope Pius XII to think of the

apostolic delegate in Turkey. Archbishop Roncalli
had a reputation for calmness in the face of the
most delicate situations, for an adaptability and
skillfulness in handling affairs, and for wise and
level-headed judgment concerning men and events.

His predecessor in the nunciature in France, until a few months previously, had been Archbishop
(now Cardinal) Valerio Valeri. The religious interests of France had demanded that he follow the
government of Marshal Pétain south after the
German occupation, and establish himself in the
capital of unoccupied France at Vichy. Many
other members of the diplomatic corps did the
same. Thus, when Paris and a large part of France
had been reconquered by the Allies, Nuncio
Valeri's position became embarrassing. A diplomat
accredited to a government whose members were
now in disgrace could hardly be acceptable to the
new government of liberation which was preparing to bring charges against the "Vichy collaborators." [2]

On the morning of January 1, the new papal
nuncio and, *ex officio,* dean of the diplomatic
corps, presented to General de Gaulle the best
wishes of the diplomatic corps for the new year.
Since de Gaulle's provisional government had been
in power scarcely four months, these were the first

[2] Archbishop Valeri, who had succeeded Luigi Maglione in
the Paris nunciature when the latter was named cardinal, had
long been in the Orient, like Roncalli, as representative of the
Holy See. Both Valeri and Roncalli were elevated to the purple
by Pius XII on January 12, 1953, to the general satisfaction of
the now pacified French.

formal diplomatic representations which the new government of France had received; they were made while the cannons were still booming on the frontier.

The address which the nuncio delivered on this occasion was a masterpiece of soberness, cordiality and common sense:

It is a great honor for me to speak for the first time to Your Excellency on behalf of my eminent colleagues in the diplomatic corps, and to express, in the name of our sovereigns and heads of state, our wishes for the new year.

In the midst of trials and unavoidable sufferings, the year which has just passed has been marked by events of greatest importance for France. Thanks to your political vision and energy, this dear country has refound, as it were, its liberty and faith in its destiny.

We do not doubt that this coming year will witness new progress and new heights. France is now resuming its traditional physiognomy and the place which belongs to it among the nations. With its lucid mind, its love of work, its love of liberty, its spiritual influence —of which I have myself been the happy witness during many long years in the Near East—it will be able to show the way which, by a union of hearts and in justice, will lead our society at last toward a period of enduring peace and tranquility. This is the invitation which comes from on high during these days. May it be well received by all men of good will.

These are our wishes and our hopes, Mr. President. To which we add our best wishes for your personal welfare in calling on Divine Providence to preserve you long in the affection of your country.

Paris

The French attacked the immense problem of the moral, spiritual and social rebirth of their country with their customary energy. In a country which was adopting a new constitution, seeking new political and social paths, and in which a new governing class was coming to the fore, Nuncio Roncalli had many opportunities to demonstrate his skill, his experience, his gracious and friendly manner, and his human and Christian kindliness. He sought to be an example to all and a stimulus to Catholics, in order to bring about that concord of spirits which the hour demanded. Thus he succeeded in demonstrating brilliantly that, far from being incompatible, the nation and its religious institutions could mutually and simultaneously experience a rebirth and a rejuvenation.

The addresses which he delivered at the Elysée as dean of the diplomatic corps, while presenting the latter's greeting each new year to the president of the republic, provide the best illustration of his tact and Christian awareness. He touched upon the principal themes of the hour with particular reference to the mission and responsibility of France.

On New Year's Day in 1949, he underlined the importance of the United Nations for the attainment of peace and guarding the fundamental rights of man and the citizen:

The road which leads to peace, it is true, is still very rough and difficult. Above all, it should be smoothed by the spontaneous recognition and individual and collective enjoyment of liberty, of liberty in all countries, the daughter of God and imprescriptible right of man and the citizen.

Alas! Too often it is the groaning of suppressed liberty which reaches our ears from various points in the world—not to admit this would be an unpardonable hypocrisy on my part; namely, the voices of millions of men who, obliged to flee from their native homes, wander about the world in search of a corner where they may build a modest home, voices which break our heart and fill our souls with darkness. . . .

Mr. President, we wish to share your vigilance and defend our optimism as you do.

During these last months, Paris, the crossroad of Europe, and even of the world, has had the honor of being host, with its characteristic hospitality, to the great assembly of the United Nations gathered for the planning of world peace.

All questions have, of course, not been resolved, nor did anyone think that it was possible to complete such an immense task. But the debates have gradually assumed a calmer tone. Several important principles have been affirmed which are worthy of respect, for they correspond to the fundamental rights of man and the citizen, with the result that in view of the innumerable words spoken at the UN during the course of these three months, we can apply the precept of St. Paul: "Test all things; hold fast to that which is good" (1 Thess. 5:21).

Now what is most important is to find a way to make words and facts agree in a spirit of sincerity; it is the constant determination of statesmen and diplomats to promote justice and fraternity among nations even at the expense of particular preoccupations which may happen to be fully justified in themselves.

Paris

On New Year's Day in 1950, after summarizing the moral balance of the first fifty years of the twentieth century, he predicted better times for the second half, which was beginning under the pacific auspices of the great Jubilee Year:

In the course of the last year when the Council of Europe met for the first time at Strasbourg, the noble and forceful words of the president of the French National Assembly made all hearts ring. Recalling this saying of the Philosopher of the North: "Politics must bend the knee before morality," he warmly urged the members to study the most difficult problems of international society, a study destined to realize—these are the very words Monsieur Herriot—"a large part of the most lofty ideal which has ever been proposed to delegations: Peace on earth to men of good will."

May a humble apostolic nuncio in France, a nation always faithful to its glorious tradition of being an intelligent and tireless herald of justice and peace in the world, be permitted, Mr. President, to echo this speech at Strasbourg and to point, as a symbol of greater favor in the future, to the door of God's great pardon and the reconciliation of men which has been opened during these last few days among the nations.

The masses with their ancient faith will pass through it, exulting in their invincible hope—*spes invicta credentium*—the sons of France, ever and always in the front ranks. For all the others this door will at least be a sign of optimism worthy of profound reflection and respect. Through it people shall pass, like the gate in the Bible *ad viam ascensionis,* not in order to descend but to ascend. On the spiritual level, this is

75

the vocation of individuals and peoples: not to decline, but to rise ever upward. . . .

During 1951 he spoke of the duties of diplomats in dealing with the problems of nations (this was a few months before the outbreak of the Korean War):

To pass a year of one's life as a diplomat in Paris is a rare and enviable privilege. But it is not our task, as I see it, to confine ourselves in this capital to the simple enjoyment of pleasures of the spirit amidst such richness and fascinating history, art, thought, and life; but to accomplish the grave and weighty tasks which are the typical lot of those in our position in the face of such vast and profound world problems. . . .

Now, once again, the mournful image of war—of war "detested by mothers"—has begun to reappear, interrupting the spell and placing people—all people —face to face with a reality which makes them tremble. . . .

Now war is the subversion of every civilization: it is the return to barbarism. Even when the necessity of resisting violence—*vim vi repellere*—the defense of security or fundamental liberties make it unavoidable, war ought always to be the *ultima ratio*.

Before reaching that point, it is the task of diplomacy, at all costs, to explore every means whereby war can be avoided.

The work of diplomacy is one of the most noble and precious services which a citizen can be called on to fulfill for the needs and advantage of his country; a service which knows no respite, inspired by the fear of

God and true love of men, calling for wisdom, calmness and constancy.

Finally the address which he delivered on New Year's Day in 1952 was a masterpiece of finesse. He took as his text one of the fables of La Fontaine, in order to recall the glorious mission of France:

This year I have been inspired by the last pages of a small book, a gem of your literature of the *Grand Siècle* which, imbued with the wisdom of the ancient world, has done so much to make known throughout the world the depth, delicacy, and charm of the French mind: the *Fables* of La Fontaine.

In the last of them, entitled " The Judge, the Hospitaller, and the Solitary," three saints are seeking a way to salvation. Everything is obvious: persons, principles, and characters. We are all represented there, governors, politicians, diplomats. . . . The Judge thought that he could succeed with his work of reconciliation. But "no one was content." Is this not true of these last few months? We have had innumerable international meetings, but the results have been meager, even disillusioning.

The second of our saints, the Hospitaller, devotes himself to what we would call today public assistance, social work. The Judge goes to see him and finds that he is also rewarded only with "complaints and murmurs"; people accuse him of injustice and partiality!

They both then go to the third, a Solitary, who lives "under rough rocks, near a pure spring," and they ask his advice. "They must," he tells them, "find

77

this out for themselves. Who better than they can know what their needs are? To learn to know oneself is the first of cares which the Supreme Majesty has imposed on each mortal." And he adds: "Trouble the water and do you see yourself? . . . Leave it alone and you will then see your image." The poet adds: "Thus spoke the Solitary, he was believed and they followed this salutary advice."

Please God that this doctrine of "Know Thyself"— *Nosce te ipsum*—inscribed above the door of the Temple of Delphi and which is applicable to all, may be understood and widely put into practice everywhere that responsibility is being exercised for the common good, everywhere that people are conscious of the gravest problem of the hour: that of saving peace, saving it at any price.

With such thoughts in mind it is permissible to look toward the new year with hope. We hope that it may be prosperous and happy for you, Mr. President; for your distinguished collaborators, who, according to La Fontaine, "bear the public weal, magistrates, princes and ministers"; and for immortal France.

Will you find other difficulties along the way, new sources of anxiey? Never fear, the motto of the city of Paris should always be before your eyes: *Fluctuat nec mergitur,* a motto of calmness and confidence, of safe passage through the waters of the centuries.

May a humble apostolic nuncio, charged with the responsibility of representing the highest principles of the spiritual order which justify the honor given him of expressing the sentiments of the diplomatic corps on this solemn occasion of the New Year, be permitted to raise up with him the eyes and hearts of all toward the star which shines over the troubled waters and to read in the light of the heavens the words which are so characteristic of the history and life of France: *Gesta Dei, Gesta Dei!* Each nation has its destiny in the hidden designs of Providence, and each helps the other to realize it. Preserving a strong faith, an invincible optimism and a heart open to genuine effusions of human and Christian brotherhood, we all have the right to fear nothing and to have confidence in the aid of God, for the France of today and tomorrow, always faithful to its glorious tradition, a benefaction and encouragement to all nations. . . .

While he interested himself in the problems of the country and followed the evolution of its political, social and religious condition, Nuncio Roncalli was also careful to avoid any interference in the internal affairs of France. This attitude on his part was recognized by all but the prejudiced. The statesman Maurice Schumann declared of him: "On the eve of Monseigneur Roncalli's departure from France, some question concerning him was raised in the National Assembly by a deputy who was more slow-witted than ill-willed. I was then secretary of state for foreign affairs, and had the honor of defending the nuncio in the name of the government. The following day Monseigneur Roncalli said to me: 'I want to thank you for your kind words. I thank you particularly for not having said anything offensive against the one who raised the question.' This natural repudiation of intolerance and violence on his part, is this not, in the cruel age in which we live, the most necessary virtue for the highest spiritual authority in the world?"

79

We Have a Pope

The French "sympathized" immediately with the nuncio and his popularity increased proportionately as, each year, they had an opportunity to see him at numerous religious and civil ceremonies in which he took part in every corner of France and even in metropolitan France overseas.

The French press was generous with praise of him and his mission there. As a man of culture and taste, and endowed with a highly-developed critical sense, the apostolic nuncio quickly found himself at ease in Paris in the cultural world of the French capital. He sympathized with the journalists whom he frequently saw and with whom he loved to converse on all sorts of subjects, because, as he said, "I also have a great thirst to know and to keep abreast of everything."

An intimate of leading lights in the political and artistic world, he became friendly with all those noted for their brilliance of mind and integrity and whom he thought he could help spiritually, such as Herriot and Auriol.

A French journalist wrote about him under the title "A serene and enlightened Nuncio": [3] "Monseigneur Roncalli, who holds this well-known post at Paris, is always filled with optimism. Even during the harsh, dark first years of the Fourth Republic, at the time when our wounds were open and we were laying the groundwork of our moral and religious reconstruction, he exhibited a serene confidence in the destiny of our country. Cleverness? Insight? Calculated remarks? It does not

3 *Le Monde,* October 30, 1958.

matter. The fact is that he has won great sympathy in Paris even among political milieux steeped in a now pointless anticlericalism."

Before leaving Paris as nuncio he wished to see again all those men who had been heads of government during his eight years' residence in France. At a luncheon which he gave at the nunciature in February, 1953, shortly after he had received the red hat, the following premiers found themselves at table together: Edgard Faure, Georges Bidault, Antoine Pinay, René Mayer, René Pleven. "Only under my roof," the cardinal said jokingly, "can French politicians of such diverse views get together peacefully."

FOR THE CHURCH IN FRANCE

Nuncio Roncalli also had an opportunity to display his flexibility and diplomatic skill in the negotiations leading to a reconciliation between the hierarchy and the new government of the resistance, which, headed by de Gaulle, was inclined to be quite intransigent on certain questions.

The purging of political ranks was pursued ruthlessly. Many Catholics who had formed a political party (MRP) during the years of resistance were unsympathetic to any form of religious control and were hardly disposed to be tolerant of the so-called "collaborators." The drama of patriotism though which they had recently passed kept them prisoners, and certain militant Catholics were decidedly averse to any appeal to toleration, patience, or farsightedness.

The extreme Left had ably succeeded in identifying Catholicism and the Vichy regime in the public mind. The MRP also wished to defend the ideals of the new state which had emerged from the resistance; but, young and inexperienced, it could not liberate itself from the undeserved accusations and legacy which the extreme Left wished to pin on Catholics. Laicism threatened again to become a new militant anticlericalism, and even the MRP was infected.

At one point, while the MRP was in the government, a conflict broke out between the French state and the Church: the government demanded, among other things, the deposition of numerous bishops who, in its opinion, had sided too closely with the past regime and had "betrayed" France. Moreover, it put forth claims of a Gallican nature to control the activity of the clergy in the future.

It was in the midst of a situation like this that Nuncio Roncalli began his mission in France: in an atmosphere of distrust and even hostility.

He succeeded magnificently, however, in the task entrusted to him by the Holy See: of the many bishops who were to have lost their sees, only three were actually obliged to resign. French Catholicism found itself united; the hierarchy maintained its independence vis-à-vis the state, and the latter gave up its attempt to make the Church in France into a national church with schismatic tendencies. Above all there came to an end the perilous confusion which identified the activity of Catholicism with the politics of the MRP.

Patient and flexible, but tenacious, without ever allowing the accusation to be made of him that he was interfering in the internal affairs of the state, the nuncio re-established normalcy in the relations between the clergy and the civil power. His line of conduct was simple and direct: the Church must obey Rome in that which relates to its spiritual ministry, and keep itself removed from those things which are purely of a temporal nature. It was the line of balance, reality, and therefore of success.

GRAVE PROBLEMS

On January 6, 1945, Pius XII directed a letter to the French episcopate which would constitute, for the newly arrived nuncio, a basic document regarding his mission to the French church.

The pope reaffirmed in this document his confidence in the "spiritual resources" of France for finding once again in "its very disgrace an *élan* to even newer heights."

But to arrive at this it was necessary that all French Catholics, "matured by the common sufferings," should embark on the road of mutual and fraternal understanding.

It was a question—according to Pius XII—of causing a new world to arise both for France and for the other nations from the ruins of the war: "a world better organized in its juridical structure, a world more equitable, sane, in which men strive together to eliminate the most crying injustices and search for themes of fraternal *rapprochement* rather than for reasons for discord or bitterness."

The Church could count on a clergy and laity in France which had "shown by their example that, even on the human level, their devotion could rise to the point of sacrifice for liberty and life, generously given for the supreme interests of *La Patrie*."

The letter therefore welcomed the appearance in Catholic organizations of a great number of persons "firm in principle, accurately informed concerning the doctrine of the Church, dedicated to making the true Christian spirit penetrate in the social, economic, and juridical fields, to assuring, by their civic and political action, the safeguarding of religious interests."

Pius XII hoped that the family would resume its former stability and fecundity in France. He recommended to the bishops the reopening of seminaries and an increase in vocations; to the clergy, dedication to studies and action "in full wisdom" with regard to problems of the present hour, above all social problems; to the faithful, obedience to those who are called to rule the Church of God.

The papal letter recalled, finally, words that had been spoken from the pulpit of Notre Dame by the then Cardinal Pacelli: "Be faithful to your traditional vocation. Never has the hour been more grave for assuming duties, never more appropriate for answering this call. Do not let the hour pass, do not let the gifts, which God has designed for the mission which He entrusts to you, be frittered away; do not waste them, do not profane them in the service of some other deceptive ideal, uncertain or less noble or worthy of you."

Nuncio Roncalli would make it his duty to recall these apostolic ideals to the Church in France by his discreet but highly effective activity ("He is the man about whom least is said," said a French journalist, "but the one who has perhaps done most").

With those Catholic circles which were intolerant of any directives from Rome and in the face of many grave problems (the structure and tasks of French Catholic Action; the relations between Catholic peasants and workers; the question of relations with the Communists, particularly acute for the MRP and Catholic labor leaders; irenicism; integralism; the progressive de-Christianization of certain sectors of the population), the nuncio intervened, saving, at times, a situation which seemed, as in the case of the worker-priests, hopelessly compromised.

French Catholicism today, which, as we have mentioned, no longer has any reasons for conflict with the state, shows a vitality which owes nothing to politics and which is characterized by a great fervor and great activity. Its very restlessness is a sign of its vitality.

One of the French newspapers would write, after his elevation to the papacy: [4] "We rejoice that

4 *Témoignage chrétien*, October 31, 1958.

the new pope knows our country, our people, our problems. Has he not lived for eight years amongst us? He has witnessed the prodigious rise of French Catholicism from the aftermath of the war. He has followed at first hand the missionary work of Cardinal Suhard. He knows the worth of our efforts, our will to increase the influence of the Church, to make it felt in the modern world. He has equally known our sufferings and has seen us overcome so many difficulties. We met him when he was nuncio in Paris, so affable to all, so anxious to know, so foreign to intrigue and cabals."

Once he had left France for his appointment as patriarch of Venice, Cardinal Roncalli would continue to have a warm spot in his heart for it and take an interest in its problems.

When he was legate *a latere* of Pius XII for the consecration of the new underground basilica at Lourdes, in the remarkable allocution which he gave on this occasion, he said to the Blessed Virgin: "Preserve your fondness for this land of France, this glorious people through the ages, *quem coequasti Primogenito tuo.*"

Shortly after his elevation to the supreme pontificate, he sent a message to the French episcopate:

From the moment of Our elevation to the supreme pontificate, Our thoughts turned with paternal affection to members of the French episcopate, for whom We nourish great esteem and with whom We have dealt during many long years of cordial relations. We pray God to fructify their generous apostolate and send them from Our heart by means of you, as well as to their dioceses and yourselves, Our first apostolic blessing.[5]

DEVOTION TO OUR LADY OF LOURDES

The bishop of Lourdes, Pierre-Marie Théas, remembered after the election of John XXIII the love of the new pope for Our Lady of Lourdes.

The last three pontiffs, Benedict XV, Pius XI and Pius XII, had each, in turn, been pilgrims to Lourdes. John XXIII himself went to the city of Mary ten times.

As a young priest, he went there for the first time with the bishop of Bergamo, Giovanni Radini-Tedeschi, the promoter of Italian pilgrimages to the Grotto of Massabielle.

During the period of his nunciature in Paris, Archbishop Roncalli went there almost every year. In 1947 he presided over the French national pilgrimage, the principal spiritual purpose of which was to "pray for the peace of the world." On this occasion the nuncio was named honorary canon of the cathedral of Tarbes.

[5] In speaking of the apostolic solicitude of Nuncio Roncalli, we cannot fail to mention the work done by him on behalf of prisoners of war, especially Germans and displaced persons. He had the fate of priests and seminarians who were prisoners of war much at heart. As soon as he arrived in France he encouraged the formation at Chartres of a seminary for German clerical prisoners, that they might make up for the time lost during the war, and once they had returned to their dioceses, be ready for their sacred ministry. The government of the German Federal Republic conferred upon him a high honor in recognition of these services.

We Have a Pope

During the Marian Year (1954), while patriarch of Venice, Cardinal Roncalli, accompanied by all the bishops of his province, led a great regional pilgrimage to Lourdes.

He who was to succeed St. Pius X on the throne of St. Peter, after having occupied the patriarchal throne of Venice, was also the consecrator of the basilica of St. Pius X at Lourdes in March, 1958.

On March 23, upon his arrival at the airport of Tarbes, Cardinal Roncalli received an enthusiastic welcome from religious, civil, and military authorities, and above all from the people and pilgrims present at Lourdes.

The ritual of consecration took place during the days of March 24 and 25 with an incomparable splendor and majesty. The moving address which the cardinal delivered elicited an enthusiastic response from those present.

The bishop of Lourdes received, on October 26, 1958, a letter from Cardinal Roncalli which began: "At the moment of entering the conclave, my thoughts are carried to Lourdes to the Basilica of St. Pius X, and especially to the Immaculate Virgin of the Grotto."

Elected pope on October 28, he sent a telegram on November 2 to the bishop of Lourdes, as follows:

We thank you for the filial message which has come to Us from the shrine of Lourdes on the occasion of Our elevation to the throne of St. Peter; and while We entrust Our pontificate to the maternal protection of the Immaculate Virgin in this centenary year of her Apparition at Massabielle, We thank you for your prayers on behalf of Our intentions at the blessed grotto, which We have visited and which is now dearer than ever to Us because *Domus Mariæ domus Papæ.*

Lourdes, the city of the Blessed Virgin, is therefore, for John XXIII, the city of the supreme pontiff.

PERMANENT OBSERVER WITH UNESCO

In 1951 the Holy See, which had already participated, by means of delegations headed by an observer, in the General Conferences of UNESCO in Beirut, Paris, and Florence, decided to have itself represented in a more permanent fashion at the Secretariate of the Organization.

Among the specialized agencies of the United Nations, UNESCO, as a matter of fact, is that one which by its particular activities is closest to the interests of the Catholic Church.

The task of an observer was that of remaining in contact with the various "departments" (especially those concerning education, the social sciences, cultural activities, exchanges of persons) of the Secretariate; of keeping near officials to supply them with information necessary for a better understanding of Catholic principles; of following the publications printed under the auspices of UNESCO; of keeping abreast of the activities centered there; of following, finally, the work of the Catholic Center of Coordination with UNESCO.

To undertake this delicate task Pius XII chose the apostolic nuncio in France, who thus became the first permanent observer for the Holy See. In 1952, in view of the numerous important occupations which weighed on Archbishop Roncalli, he was given an assistant observer. In 1953, it was considered more appropriate to entrust the position to someone other than the apostolic nuncio.

The permanent observer who, in July, 1951, headed the delegation of the Holy See to the Sixth General Conference of UNESCO, dealt in a masterly address with the significance of Catholic participation in the activity of the organization.

He said among other things:

As representative of the most ancient and vast cultural organization in the world, called into existence under the motto: *euntes docete,* "Go and teach," which from the hills of Galilee ruffled the waves of a small lake, and which, after two thousand years, continues to be heard on all shores and in all lands where liberty is not an empty word, as this representative, it would be entirely natural to recall the great principle and great foundation: God, *Dominus scientiarum,* on whom this powerful system has been raised and from whom it derives its strength. . . .

UNESCO appeared henceforth to be not what everyone feared it might be at first, that is, a great museum destined for the intellectual or cultural distraction of a curious crowd, but as a great living hearth, the sparks of which would everywhere en-kindle energies and cooperation for the ends of jus-tice, liberty, and peace for all peoples of the earth, without distinction of race, language or religion.

Yes, without distinction of race, language or re-ligion.

If I stop here a moment to underline this clear position of UNESCO, contained in the preamble of its constitution signed in London in 1945, with respect to the relations of race, language or religion for all the nations to which its activity would extend, it is not because the racial, literary or religious values of each people are ignored or neglected. On the contrary, it is in order that these values may always be taken into proper account. UNESCO wishes to be, let us say, a higher good, a great school to be respected; but as such, it must not be blind or deaf to the fundamental values of the psychology of each people, namely, their national feeling and religious spirit.

These are the proofs of the good will of UNESCO in the face of situations and fundamental problems which assure the great organization the confidence and collaboration of the most notable part of hu-manity. . . .

Among the tasks of the present session, I mention two which are particularly important: first, the tech-nical assistance to underdeveloped countries; secondly, the creation throughout the world of regional centers for the development of basic education.

It is with a special interest that the observer for the Vatican considers the second of these initiatives which is related to what has always been and still is the most immediate and dearest concern of the Church: the educational and civilizing activity pursued by her for centuries through the intermediary of her missionaries scattered throughout the entire world. . . .

In the matter of education and particularly basic education, techniques are always progressing. What ought to determine the technique is a loftier inspiration. This inspiration the Church finds in the genuine love of souls. For all souls of good faith, it is the feeling of fraternity which shines on the face of each man as a reflection of the image of God. . . .

"To look at each other without distrust, to approach without fear, to help each other without compromising oneself": this is a good program of action for the progress of social life according to the aims of UNESCO. . . .

In November, 1952, at the Mass inaugurating the labors of the Seventh General Conference, he thus outlined to the Catholic delegates the importance and delicacy of their duty:

A particular reason to be pleased with this present meeting is an event which has taken place during these last few months, a flowering, as it were, the fruit of a happy mutual understanding: that is, the official presence of a permanent observer of the Holy See who directly and by means of the collaboration of a prelate who will assist him with the usual duties, will have the honor and opportunity of following the complex and vast movement which has called into being such energies intended for the diffusion of education, science, and culture, in the service of world peace.

This appointment of a permanent observer is a notable step foward for UNESCO. The unity of the

Catholic Church diffused throughout the world already amounts to a *rapprochement* of states for a greater cultural and political unity. . . .

Our steps toward UNESCO, from the time when this was born, followed this direction. And we intend to remain faithful to it. Our presence is intended to be a serious contribution, an encouragement, an edification.

In the fervor of the present intellectual efforts for culture, in the fever of publications of all kinds which are seen every day on the newsstands, in the shop windows, almost inundating the street of this marvelous metropolis which is Paris, and whence they spread over the world calling forth equal emulation of literary production in the most famous and noted centers, we are almost suffocated by the cry: We should live in the current of history. That would be the equivalent of saying: Do the new, the modern, the bizarre in everything and at all costs; as if more than two thousand years of history were not behind us to teach us something: as if the world were just now learning to walk.

We admit—smiling a little as we are greeted in our old age by each one carrying his sack of experiences on his shoulder—we admit in our contemporaries, younger than we, much good will and great confidence in the future.

Yes, we all find ourselves in the midst of the current of history, but not in order to undergo it, not to leave it to flow by itself but to dominate it, and direct it toward the salvation, not the shipwreck of the world. Modern inventions, techniques, application to practical life, human commerce, all this is interesting and worthy of respect. But is that enough, not for the temporal happiness of man but for the eternal felicity of his immortal soul? Fortunately, over the perilous current for whoever abandons himself to it, there is heard the word and commandment of Christ which the Church has heard since the first centuries, and which it honors and is always in the act of honoring. Jesus said to His most intimate disciples: "You are the light of the world, you are the salt of the earth." Higher than all the triumphs of human science, therefore, shines the gospel of Christ, which contains the elements of civilization. This is the faith of the Christian, of the Catholic. Working with UNESCO, the Catholic remembers this and derives from it inspiration and clarity of principles, for encouragement toward a serene, loyal and fraternal cooperation.

The ways of UNESCO in its search for the most practical means, those most capable of attaining its ideals of education, science, and universal culture, are various, luminous and multiple. One will often meet with and become confused by modern techniques; that is understandable. One can also be confused to the point of having the impression of practical inconsistency, lack of reality, or elsewhere, of languor. The Catholic can bring to these efforts his cooperation by his counsel or practical activity with that wisdom, that just proportion, that flavor, in a word, that salt of the earth, the evangelical salt of the Sermon on the Mount which maintains the realism, the savor which preserves from corruption, which assures the permanence and exquisite goodness of success.

During the last two years that Nuncio Roncalli represented the Holy See at UNESCO, he won general popularity. His cultural preparation, his researches in the field of history, his passion for

book collecting, his sense of fitness, his *bon mots,*
but above all his gentleness and goodness of soul,
won him the esteem of all.

The secretary of the Catholic Committee of
Coordination with UNESCO recalls: [6] "The oldest
ones remembered his visits to the secretariate on
the Avenue Kléber, his presence at general conferences (especially his intervention at one of
them), his addresses at Masses preceding the opening of the sessions.

"It is an honor for a great many officials of this
period (1951-1953) to have known him personally
and profited by his great learning, his mind so
generously open to international questions, his
finesse; all remembered his kind words, his
paternal greeting and the way in which he always
found a kind word appropriate for each occasion,
depending upon one's function or nationality, at
receptions at the nunciature, or in chance meetings. He wished to have everyone introduced to
him, those who occupied the lowest position as
well as the highest. To the extent that the burden
of work permitted, he would inform himself concerning the man's work, his country, his family,
his interests. . . . Catholics who are eager to
assure the benefit of a Christian presence in this

[6] One of the centers of the Conference of International
Catholic Organizations (OIC), with permanent secretariate at Fri-
bourg (Switzerland). The purpose of the center, which has its
seat at Paris, is to keep OIC informed of the activity of UNESCO
and coordinate the work of those who enjoy a consultative status
with the Organization.

great international organization have not forgotten the lines laid down by His Excellency
Monseigneur Roncalli. They have since derived
profit from them themselves. They desired and
desire that their presence may be a serious contribution, encouraging, edifying. . . ."

5. Venice

✠ ✠ ✠

CARDINAL

E ARLY in January, 1953, something happened
which turned out to have surprising consequences for Nuncio Roncalli. One morning while
he was reading the newspaper in his study at the
nunciature, as was his wont, his eye was caught by
something in *Figaro*—a photograph with the cap-
tion underneath: "The gondola of death." It was
the gondola which bore the remains of the deceased patriarch of Venice, Agostini, to the cemetery of San Michele in Isola. The nuncio looked
at it for a long while, then tore it out carefully
and filed it in his breviary. Venice had always
been a city very dear to him.

Several days later in the secret consistory of
January 12, 1953, Pius XII created the apostolic
nuncio in Paris a cardinal, together with twenty-
three other prelates.

Three days later, while he was still at the nunciature, the pope appointed him patriarch of
Venice. The appointment came as the culmina-

tion and reward for eight years of splendid service in one of the most important and difficult posts of the papal diplomatic service.

Along with his appointment as cardinal, Roncalli was assigned the titular church of Santa Prisca, one of the oldest in Rome. Cardinal Roncalli always cherished a special regard for this titular church of his, situated as it is in one of the most delightful spots on the Aventine Hill, and never failed to pay it a visit during his infrequent jaunts from Venice to Rome.

When he was asked what he thought of his appointment as cardinal and patriarch, he replied: "I hope I will not be misunderstood, but while my elevation to the cardinalate had seemed, I do not say logical, but likely, in view of my long diplomatic service, it is the appointment as patriarch of Venice which has surprised and greatly affected me. It opens up an entirely new prospect for me, namely, that of being a true shepherd of souls. I am convinced that the pastoral ministry is the most fascinating, the finest which can be entrusted to any man."

The same day on which announcement of the appointment was made in Paris, the then president of the republic, Vincent Auriol, conferred the cardinal's biretta on Nuncio Roncalli in the Elysée Palace.[1] The gesture was intended to be a

[1] The custom of conferring the "biretta" (one of the important symbols of the dignity of a cardinal) on new members of the Sacred College who find themselves outside of Rome is an

token of the esteem and admiration in which the nuncio was held, who by his example and efforts had succeeded in winning the confidence of the government and affection of the French people.

The archbishop of Paris read the papal brief of appointment and President Auriol, in the presence of President of the Council Mayer and Foreign Minister Bidault, placed the biretta on the head of the new cardinal who knelt before him on the same red *prie-dieu* which Charles X had used on the day of his coronation.

Cardinal Roncalli, dressed in scarlet robes, delivered an address in which he expressed the hope that the French would say of him, when they recalled his stay in Paris: "He was a faithful and peace-loving priest, always a true friend of France."

President Auriol replied with praise for his gifts as a man and diplomat, and for his work, adding that for these qualities the French govern-

---

old privilege granted by the Holy See to the heads of Catholic states. The ceremonial of conferring the biretta on Cardinal Roncalli had to be carefully studied by the officials of the Elysée since such a function had not taken place in France for many years. At the time when the president of the republic was Doumergue, who happened to be a Protestant, the ceremonial was altered, since the president could not himself impose the biretta: protocol provided that it should be received from him only for conferral, and then be given to the Archbishop of Paris to be placed on the head of the new "*porporato*," who at that time happened to be Nuncio Cerretti.

The ritual at the Elysée on January 15, 1953, therefore assumed a note of special solemnity as the old tradition was revived which the French people had always found so touching.

ment had requested him to confer on him the highest national honor, the Grand Cross of the Legion of Honor.

On his return from France, since he had been appointed bishop of an Italian diocese (Venice), Cardinal Roncalli hastened to swear the prescribed oath before the then president of Italy, Luigi Einaudi, in accordance with the concordat between the Holy See and Italy.[2] The conferring of the red hat by the pope took place at Castelgandolfo on October 21, 1953.[3]

ENTRANCE INTO VENICE

The new patriarch made his entrance into Venice on March 15, 1953. He was now seventy-one years old. He became the forty-fourth patri-

[2] Strictly speaking, practice required that the oath should have been preceded by the conferring of the "red hat" (*galero*) and cardinal's ring by the pope; but Pius XII's state of health would not permit the ceremonial being performed during the time when Cardinal Roncalli was in Rome. In order not to delay him from taking formal possession of his new see, a special dispensation was granted by Pius XII in virtue of which the cardinal was able to swear the oath prescribed by the concordat in the Quirinal.

[3] It seems that Pius XII, recovering from his indisposition, waited some months before proceeding to the "little consistory," in the hope that he could bestow the red hat on the cardinals of the "Church of Silence" also, who had been created in the consistory of January 12, 1953: Archbishops Wyszyński and Stepinac. They were impeded, respectively, by the Polish and Yugoslav governments from exercising their jurisdiction. Thus this hope proved to be illusory. It was therefore natural that Pius XII should want to keep the ceremonial as austere as possible in view of the situation of the Church in communist countries.

arch and one hundred and eighty-ninth bishop of the Queen of the Adriatic.

Venice greeted him with a surge of warmth and affection. The whole city manned the embankments and bridges which line the Grand Canal. The palaces were hung with rich brocades, tapestries and damasks. Thousands upon thousands of hands waved him a heart-felt greeting along the Canal.

The cardinal made his triumphal progress through the canals of the City of the Doges aboard a motor launch of the Admiralty, between rows of launches, gondolas, and small boats of every description, which had come for the most part from the islands of the lagoon.

At the mole of the basin of San Marco the cardinal kissed the crucifix and, after having replied with paternal words to the address of the mayor, proceeded to the basilica which contains the body of the Evangelist. He then entered the church that was henceforth to be his cathedral.

The words which he addressed to the faithful on this his first occasion of meeting them were extremely simple and moving:

I was born of poor parents. . . . Providence willed that I should leave my native land and travel over the highways of the world, from East to West, bringing me into contact with serious political and social problems. Now, at the end of my long experience, Providence has placed me here in Venice, between land and sea, in a city familiar to my ancestors and to me in my studies. . . . For charity's sake, do not look upon your patriarch as a politician or diplomat, but consider him as the servant of God, the shepherd of souls called to exercise his ministry among the humble, a pastor completely unworthy of the Great Shepherd and him who represents Him on earth. Even when I was in touch with the highest persons I never dreamed of anything else. . . . O Blessed Pius X, here am I at the place that was yours.

PASTORAL ACTIVITY

As patriarch, Cardinal Roncalli also assumed the functions of metropolitan of Venice for the suffragan dioceses of Padua, Verona, Vicenza, Treviso, Feltre-Belluno, Chioggia, Concordia, Vittorio Veneto, and Adria, and of president of the Conference of Bishops of the Three Venices, comprising, besides the dioceses mentioned above, the metropolitan sees of Udine and Gorizia, the diocese of Trieste and Capodistria, the archdiocese of Trent and diocese of Bressanone.

The predecessor of Roncalli, Patriarch Carlo Agostini, had been a pious and strict individual, tireless in his activity, requiring the utmost from everybody. It therefore appeared strange to many that a diplomat should be chosen to carry on his work. But Cardinal Roncalli passed from the foreign service of the Holy See to his pastoral duties with the greatest of ease. This was another proof of the remarkable versatility which all realized that he possessed.

During the five years in which he governed the diocese, he visited the various parishes many times. He would first celebrate Mass early in the morning and then preach at all the other Masses. He would then go to the parish office and inspect the archives very carefully. He liked to be present at examinations in catechism, during which he would "converse" with the children. His examinations were never like those which one would commonly understand by the term, because he did not wish the children to be afraid of their bishop. He had words of exhortation for the clergy, even when he had to draw their attention to certain things that required correction. This he always did with great circumspection and tact, out of hearing of the laity, and also their own household servants. He would go into the kitchen to thank the women who took care of the parish residence, a gesture which he had in common with his predecessor, St. Pius X. At dinner he would speak freely without discussing business. Afternoons were devoted to visits to convents and schools, and especially to hospitals. Then he would return to the parish church and would generally preside over a parish meeting. He wished to know about the various activities and took an interest in the buildings from a liturgical and historical point of view. Finally, he was particularly glad whenever vespers could be sung by the people.

His name is linked with many important events. From November 24 to 27, 1957, he held the thirty-first diocesan synod in which he laid down rules of pastoral behavior for his clergy. He solemnized the Marian Year of 1954, and in

1956, the fifth centenary of the death of the first patriarch of Venice, St. Laurence Justinian. On that occasion he wished the pontifical Mass to be celebrated in San Marco by the archbishop of Milan, Giovanni Battista Montini. The latter has recalled that he had promised himself that he would not accept invitations to perform ceremonies or make speeches outside his own diocese, for his duties demanded all his time. However, he made an exception on this occasion for the patriarch of Venice, to whom he was bound by ties of esteem and friendship. Archbishop Montini also dedicated the new minor seminary, which he had generously helped to provide for.

The confidence which the Holy See reposed in Cardinal Roncalli, as well as his own devotion, sometimes took him outside his diocese. In 1954 he made a pilgrimage to Lourdes as head of the Venetian episcopate. He combined with this a visit to Spain as a pilgrim to the Shrine of St. James of Compostella. At the end of the same year, Pius XII sent him as legate to the National Marian Congress in Beirut, where he solemnly crowned the icon of Our Lady of Lebanon. In 1958, again as papal legate, he consecrated the underground basilica of St. Pius X at Lourdes, winning the approval of France and the whole world, especially by the speech which he made on this occasion. He then said, among other things, turning toward the Blessed Virgin: "I dare to present to you the beloved sons of my Venice, which has been delighted by the honor shown, in the person of their humble patriarch, to the beloved and famous diocese of which St. Pius X was shepherd and father, and the numerous and individual intentions which they have laid upon me. I recommend all to your loving and maternal devotion."

The patriarch was also able to complete many projects during the brief period of his rule. Besides the minor seminary mentioned above, he also built about thirty parish churches. He invited the Somaschi Fathers to Mestre and entrusted to them the shrine of the Immaculate Heart of Mary. He saw to it that the houses where the canons lived, near the patriarchal basilica, were suitably redecorated and made improvements on the basilica itself, in the crypt of which he placed the remains of his predecessors. Meanwhile he provided a new and more suitable building for the patriarchal archives and acquired the historic site of San Giorgio in Alga.

He always sought to strengthen the bond between the mainland and the City of the Lagoon and used to love to say: "I stand for that which unifies and seek to keep far off whatever divides."

Particular attention was devoted to Catholic Action. It is, in his opinion, an absolutely indispensable adjunct of the apostolate in modern times. He made a point of always being present at social, cultural, and recreational gatherings, at which he spoke in his usual engaging fatherly manner. It was said at Venice: "Our patriarch goes everywhere and nothing escapes him."

He also frequently delivered speeches outside

of Venice: at the Eucharistic or Marian Congresses of Turin (1953), Lecce (1957), Padua (1954 and 1958), Belluno (1956), Vicenza (1957), Verona (1958), Faenza (1958), Palermo (September, 1957, for an "Eastern Christian Week"), Lodi (September 20, 1958, for the eighth centenary of the reconstruction of the city). The celebration at Castelfranco of the centenary of the sacerdotal ordination of St. Pius X in the summer of 1958 placed the seal on his pastoral activity before he himself mounted the throne of St. Peter. It was Patriarch Roncalli's idea and determination which brought about this commemoration. Surrounded by the Venetian episcopate, he delivered a sermon which may be considered the last chapter in his inspiring episcopal career.

As a pastor, Cardinal Roncalli also showed that he was fully alive to social problems and did not hide his sympathy for militant Venetian Catholics in this field.

At Venice he continued his tradition of hospitality which had been so dear to him in the diplomatic service of the Holy See. Every bishop or prelate who happened to be passing through Venice was invited to be his guest at the patriarchal palace, for—as he used to say—on the day of his consecration each new bishop is admonished, in the words of St. Paul, to be *hospitalis et benignus*. Hence, while he was fond of entertaining at his table the local Venetian clergy, he also loved to invite cardinals and bishops to be his guests and to celebrate pontifical Mass or deliver sermons in his cathedral. Among those who passed through Venice and were his guests were Cardinals Siri, Lercaro, Agagianian, Feltin, Gilroy, Ottaviani, the late Cardinal Costantini, and many other bishops and prelates. Moreover, he arranged to have the panegyric of St. Mark delivered each year by a Venetian bishop.

HIS DAILY ROUTINE

The secret which enabled him to work so hard and accomplish so much, for a man of his years, apart from his zeal as patriarch for the care of souls, was the schedule he kept.

His secretary, Msgr. Loris Capovilla, reports that the cardinal's day usually began about 4:00 A.M. with prayer, the recitation of the breviary, and spiritual reading. Then followed at seven his daily Mass. At eight the cardinal took a cup of milk and a little fruit. Then he began on his correspondence, cast an eye over the daily newspapers which had been underlined for the important articles. From ten until one he granted audiences. After lunch and a visit to the Blessed Sacrament, he reserved a half-hour for rest, then began work again. He presided over diocesan commissions or received the employees of the curia and parish clergy of the diocese. At 7:45 he recited one of the three parts of the rosary with his immediate entourage, reserving the other two for private recitation. At eight in the evening came supper, after which four long strolls in the corridors of the palace, and then, after a brief interlude in his study and a visit to the church, rest at about 10:00 P.M.

This was the usual schedule of the patriarch, but he was not a slave to it. He had no compunction about departing from routine if there were sufficient pastoral or other reasons to justify it. Sometimes the cardinal would remain in his study without interruption from nine until four in the morning to prepare a pastoral or a sermon or to examine a book. In such cases the only rest he allowed himself was from four until about 7:30. Sometimes he withdrew to his bedroom even before nine, but he would resume work at one in the morning and do whatever reading or study was necessary.

He never failed to take part each year in the spiritual exercises with his fellow bishops of the province, a tradition that had been inaugurated by Cardinal La Fontaine and which he was pleased to continue.

He also took part, without fail, in the monthly retreats and meetings of the Venetian clergy.

As a pastor of souls his preferred reading was: Holy Scripture, the Fathers of the Church, the great French orators, the Spanish mystics, Church history, the lives of the saints, and liturgical and pastoral works.

AN OPTIMISTIC PATRIARCH

A separate chapter deals with the appearance and personality of John XXIII. A few incidents and characteristic traits of his stay in Venice may be recalled here to reveal the nature of the man who was called by the Venetians their "Optimistic Patriarch."

He loved Venice and the Venetians as a "precious inheritance entrusted to him by Divine Providence." The day after his election as supreme pontiff he wished first of all to receive in audience the auxiliary of Venice, to whom he said with great emotion: "All my Venetians are with me here in my heart. I bless them and I hope that I shall see them here on the day of my coronation."

Always greatly devoted to the Holy See himself, he never failed to recommend to his clergy and the faithful obedience to papal instructions. He was particularly glad, therefore, not for the esteem in which his person was held, but for the honor to his diocese, when Pius XII sent him an autograph letter in 1954 on the occasion of the fiftieth anniversary of his ordination as a priest.

He was wont to repeat that in pastoral affairs it was a question of: *Omnia videre, multa dissimulare, pauca corrigere* (See everything, overlook much, correct a few things), according to the old adage: *Multæ leges pessima res publica* (Where the laws are many the state is badly governed). He used to add: "One should order to be done only what one has some grounds for believing will be done."

He granted audiences freely. His visitor was always made to feel that there was time for expressing whatever he wished to say, while the patriarch listened patiently or showed sympathy. Even when he was obliged to say "No," he did so clearly but with grace, later turning the conversation to pleasant or edifying thoughts in order to suggest a higher view of things. He was frequently fond of showing visitors the rooms of St. Pius X and of recalling things connected with the life of the saint which he knew from personal experience as a seminarian or young priest. He thought—and frequently said so—that good conversation and a courteous manner may serve to lead souls to converse with God. In fact it was said of him, on several occasions, that his simple presence sufficed to evoke thoughts of faith.

The Venetians knew that they would be received by him standing when they entered his study in the patriarchate, and that they would find themselves before a man of wide experience and pleasing conversation who would gladly talk about his own experiences, and would frequently refer to "his" bishop Radini-Tedeschi, to whom he felt bound by devotion and whose small book of maxims and recollections always lay on his desk.

He was always master of himself, even in painful circumstances involving intimate friends and associates, for whom he suffered with the affection that always bound him to those dearest to him. The motto which came to his lips on such occasions was: *Voluntas Dei, pax nostra.*

It was not his custom to go out walking. But when it was necessary for him to go to a church or an institution or hospital, he always preferred to go out dressed simply in a black cassock without any sign of his dignity.

SOME ANECDOTES

In order to be able to build the minor seminary in the city, Patriarch Roncalli thought it proper to cede to the Filippine Institutes (now run by the Brethren of the Christian Schools) the splendid Villa Fietta, a property of the patriarchate situated at Paderno del Grappa, and used as a seminary by his predecessor.

Now, Cardinal Roncalli not only allowed, but even encouraged, by his friendly manner, everyone to express what he thought, even about those things which concerned the governing of the diocese. Thus, when he had decided to move the seminary from Villa Fietta to Venice, a "frank country gentleman" who, of course, would have preferred that the seminary remain in his neighborhood if only to allow himself the pleasure of visiting with the patriarch when he came there, tried to persuade Cardinal Roncalli to change his mind. He could not understand why the cardinal had given up a place which allowed him a restful sanctuary with a magnificent view and an ideal climate. Citing the great humanists and poets who were enamored of this lovely countryside, he pictured to his patriarch the joys of pursuing his favorite studies in the placid solitude of the villa, within sight of the beloved Madonnina del Grappa.

The patriarch replied that while he appreciated the gentleman's arguments, other things must also be considered:

"As a matter of fact, I sleep perfectly well in Venice. . . . More important are the seminary and the needs of the diocese.

"You see," he added in a friendly way, as if compelled to give an explanation, "I have few priests in my diocese where needs are constantly growing. That fine group of professor-priests, intelligent, prepared, zealous and dynamic—some of them are quite young—would have to be at Villa Fietta, if the minor seminary were to remain at Paderno [about fifty miles from Venice]. Thus, they could not give me that precious help which they can and do give, residing in Venice at the parish churches. I repeat: what counts is the salvation of souls."

The canons of Venice, even the honorary ones, are almost all from the city. The parish clergy of the small peripheral parishes, situated on the more remote islands or on stretches of the mainland, necessarily have less contact with the city (in Venice everything moves more slowly than on the mainland since the roads are canals and one cannot get about as one can on highways) and are therefore less well known. But Patriarch Roncalli frequently visited all the parishes in his charge, even the smallest and most remote, either by motor launch or small boat, and he knew personally all the pastors and their assistants. In 1956, on the way to a ceremony designating some new canons of the cathedral of San Marco, he mentioned to some of the dignitaries about him that he was also making Marco Polo a canon.

Noticing the surprise of some to whom this utterance seemed strange, he added the explanation in a jovial tone: "Marco Polo, the glory of Venice, made Venice and Europe known to China and China to Europe. But I naturally am referring to another Marco Polo, also a Venetian, a vigorous and zealous parish priest who has been for years not in China but in the lagoon, where I found him. He does much honor to the diocese and deserves to be honored."

The parish priest of Burano (the Island of Lace), today a canon and a monsignor, has the name of Marco Polo.

The patriarch quickly became popular at Venice. His kindliness was of the same kind as that of the quick-witted Venetian people. One day after his entrance, he wished to take a walk to the public gardens—something rare for him—with his secretary. He intended to return by the same means, but the paved streets of Venice are not country roads, and, once he had arrived at the gardens, the tired patriarch decided to take a steam launch back. He sat down among the passengers and as those nearby kissed his ring, he began to engage in conversation; people crowded around him from all sides, pleasantly surprised that he was so easy to approach; they even escorted him to San Marco in order to have the pleasure of hearing what he had to say on the way.

Anecdotes were soon circulating concerning him, as during the patriarchate of Sarto, later Pius X. It is said that he once comforted a very fat man who was all worn out by telling him: "The Lord will have to have patience with us who are fat."

Another time he told his secretary who had given 100 lire to a poor man, that in order to be worth something, the lire should now have been 1,000. "It was not proper to devaluate charity along with money!"

Those who thought that the new patriarch would be an easygoing and amiable pastor ("The calm after the storm," they had said of him, comparing him to his predecessor Agostini) soon had their illusions dispelled. The methods of both were quite different, but Patriarch Roncalli also required that all should give their utmost, although he handled them gently, and had clear ideas about what he wanted, as well as the experience and energy to get done what he intended should be done.

The patriarch also wished to open the doors of San Marco to contemporary sacred music. In September, 1956, in the cathedral of Venice, were heard the ultramodern notes of a concerto by Stravinsky in honor of St. Mark, written by the composer "in full humility before the Catholic Church." In September, 1958, the patriarch was present at the general rehearsal of Stravinsky's *Lamentationes Jeremiæ Prophetæ* when the Russian composer came to Venice to be present at the performance of his latest work. Persons close to Cardinal Roncalli said that he was profoundly moved by the sorrowful poetry of the *Job* and the *Ecclesiastes*.

The patriarch also made a point of visiting the Biennial Exhibition of the Arts of Design in 1958, breaking with a long tradition, and taking an interest in the works shown there. "Art," he said, "is neither pagan nor Christian; it derives its significance from the idea which inspires it."

6. Habemus Papam

✤ ✤ ✤

LEAVING VENICE

THE EARTHLY life of Pius XII came to an end on October 9, 1958, after a pontificate of nearly twenty years. The choice of a successor appeared to be particularly difficult, in view of the remarkable gifts of mind and spirit with which Pius had adorned the Apostolic See, the loftiness and breadth of his teaching, the many important events which had taken place in the life of the Church during his reign.

The fifty-four cardinals at once began to gather from the four quarters of the globe—all, that is, with the exception of Cardinal Mindszenty, Archbishop of Esztergom, who dwells in political asylum at the American Legation in Budapest, and Cardinal Stepinac, Archbishop of Zagreb, who has been confined to his native village of Krasic by the Yugoslav government—according to the terms of the apostolic constitution which regulates a vacancy in the Apostolic See, to be present at the funeral of the deceased pontiff and take part in the conclave for the election of his successor.

The morning of October 12, Patriarch Cardinal Roncalli also left Venice, amidst signs of the great affection which the people bore him. Before embarking on the motor launch which was to take him to the station, the patriarch visited San Marco to recite the usual prayers for a journey before the altar of the Evangelist. Then he prayed briefly before the Blessed Sacrament and the miraculous image of the madonna called the Nicopœia.

All along the way to the station, from the mole of San Marco and along the banks of the Grand Canal, the crowds showed their affection for him. Others groups gathered at the station and made the hall ring with shouts of *"Evviva."*

Entering the compartment which had been reserved for him, the cardinal went to the window and to those who wished him well for his trip and the conclave, he kept saying: "The one wish for me is to be able to return to Venice within a fortnight." Before leaving for Rome he had sent a letter to the "Sons of the Patriarchate" to thank the clergy and laity of the diocese for their manifestation of sorrow and tribute to the memory of Pius XII. The letter concluded with an invitation to the faithful to "accompany him with their prayers that the modest and very humble contribution which the cardinal of the title of Santa Prisca and Patriarch of Venice could make by way of counsel and cooperation in the coming conclave for the election of a new pope might have results consoling to Holy Church and profitable to souls."

Cardinal Patriarch Giuseppe Sarto, when leaving for the conclave on July 24, 1903, from which he was to emerge as Pius X, had also expressed the wish to his flock that he "might return soon."

WAITING FOR THE CONCLAVE IN ROME

Arriving in Rome, he found another group waiting at the station to welcome him warmly. His friends in the curia, Bergamasks and Venetian residents of Rome, people of all stations, had arranged to be there for the purpose. He was genuinely surprised and inquired whether it was customary for so many people to wait for the arrival of every cardinal. When a prelate from the Secretariate of State replied rather wittily that the demonstrations were twice as strong for him because he was both a cardinal and a patriarch, he smiled at this explanation and then proceeded to pass through the crowd, bestowing his blessing with that usual kindness which always inpresses those who are near.

At Rome he took up lodgings in the *Domus Mariæ* of the Women's Catholic Action, choosing this rather remote place purposely, because it was far from the center of the city and from those rumors which were circulating at the time. To those who brought word that he himself was being

119

talked of as a possible successor for Pius XII, he would invariably reply by repeating the ancient adage: "He who enters the conclave a pope, comes out a cardinal." Even on the eve of the conclave, when someone expressed the wish that he would be elected, he pointed to the crucifix on the wall of his simply-furnished room and said: "The papacy is a road to Calvary to be crucified with Christ."

During the days immediately preceding the conclave he lived as retired an existence as possible, receiving no formal visits, and excusing himself to his friends on the grounds of the circumstances. Photographers and, particularly, newspapermen were, by his orders, courteously but firmly shown to the door.

Still he wished to see once again the sites in Rome to which he was bound by various moments in his life: the church of Santa Maria in Monte Santo where he had been ordained priest long before in August, 1904; the altar by the tomb of St. Peter where he had celebrated his first Mass; and finally the church of San Carlo al Corso, where he had been consecrated bishop. He also made a visit to the Chiesa Nuova to venerate the body of St. Philip Neri, the saint whose spirituality was so dear to him. After pausing briefly for prayer before the urn, he expressed the wish to be able to visit the grave of Cardinal Cesare Baronius, reminding those present how the famous disciple of St. Philip used to go every day to visit the basilica of St. Peter to kiss the foot of the bronze statue of the first pope as a sign of his loyalty and obedience to the Apostolic See. With regard to Baronius, Cardinal Roncalli added that his motto had been *Obœdientia et pax,* the motto which he himself had chosen.

From the *Domus Mariæ* he wrote two letters of greeting. Both were dated October 17. In them he took occasion to make certain observations on the conclave which reveal the thoughts with which he had prepared himself for the election of the pope and which remain a testimonial to his spirituality. The first letter, addressed to the bishop of Bergamo, Giuseppe Piazzi, was as follows:

Most Reverend and Dear Excellency, a word about my entering the conclave. I seem to be making an invocation, by the mouth of a bishop, to all that is dearest to my heart as a good son of Bergamo. In thinking of all the venerated and beloved images of Mary spread throughout the diocese, with the memory of our patron saints and bishops, and illustrious priests and saints, both religious men and women of such outstanding virtue, the soul finds comfort in the confidence of the new Pentecost which will give a Holy Church in the renewal of its Head and in the reconstruction of the ecclesiastical framework a new vigor toward the victory of truth, goodness and peace. It matters little whether the new pope be from Bergamo or not. Our common prayers should be to obtain as pope a man who will be a wise and gentle governor, a saint and a sanctifier. Your Excellency understands what I mean. Greetings and my hearty embrace. A blessing also for all your little sons.

We Have a Pope

The second letter, addressed to the rector of the seminary in Venice, contained, among other things, the following thoughts:

As for the pope who has died and ascended to glory, it only remains to continue the acclamation: Long live the pope! and to pray that his successor, whoever he may be, may not represent a break in continuity, but progress in following the eternal youth of Holy Church, whose mission is always that of being a leader of souls to the divine heights of evangelical realization and sanctification of human life with a view to eternal life. It is true that the material world makes progress with its discoveries calculated to provide greater comforts for the living, but its progress counts for nothing, no more than the proverbial straw which is ignited by a spark and reduced to the merest ash.

Now I am about to enter the conclave and bear with me the face of the Madonna della Salute, and the image of my dear seminarians with whom I intend to work even more closely and devotedly as soon as I return to Venice, in a common effort of father and sons to achieve even greater heights of dedication, application and self-sacrifice.

I should not fail to mention that I count greatly on the prayers of my seminarians, whom together with their worthy superiors, here from the tomb of St. Peter who called Mark his son: *Salutat vos Ecclesia . . . et filius Marcus filius meus,* I embrace and bless.

Habemus Papam

Saturday, October 25, the day on which the conclave was opened, began with a votive Mass of the Holy Ghost celebrated at the altar of the Chair in St. Peter's by the Cardinal-Dean Eugène Tisserant. The cardinals entered the basilica in procession from the sacristy, escorted by nobles and the Swiss Guard. After homage to the Blessed Sacrament, they proceeded to the apse for the Mass. When the sacred rites had been concluded, the secretary of briefs to princes, Msgr. Antonio Bacci, delivered the traditional homily *De eligendo Summo Pontifice* in Latin. His speech, outlining a new program for an apostolate, contained among other passages the following:

When Pius XII mounted the throne of St. Peter, humanity was on the verge of being overwhelmed by a dreadful and destructive war. We must also recognize that the present time is no less uncertain and grave with perils. War has ceased, but the causes which contributed toward it have not been settled. The reason for this is evident: men are able to prepare for war, but they cannot give themselves true peace unless they are inspired by the teaching of the gospel according to which man is not, as Plautus said, "a wolf among other wolves," but a brother.

The new pontiff therefore should have the gifts necessary to cause the light and goodness of Christ to penetrate into minds and all ranks of society, that there may not rise up a new Cain who will dare to stain the soil with fratricidal blood.

123

Moreover, in many nations famous for their history or their cultural and scientific progress, religion, which is the only sure and indestructible foundation of human law and human partnership, is either forgotten or set aside, or—what is worse—is persecuted in the most insidious and inhuman manner. Priests, bishops and even members of the Sacred College are either in prison or have been banished or impeded from fulfilling their sacred ministry.

For this reason we have need of a pontiff endowed with great strength of mind together with an ardent charity; of a pontiff who knows how to tell the truth even to those who do not wish to hear it; who knows how to defend the rights of Christian and human civilization, but at the same time to open the arms of pardon to all, even to those who make bloody the heart of the common Father and who try to darken the path of civilization by denying the primary rights of human liberty.

Moreover, he must be a *teacher* to all, ever ready to unmask and condemn errors wherever they may occur. While a frivolous, impudent, and sometimes even sacrilegious and mercenary press seeks to poison minds and pervert the hearts and morals especially of the young, while in many countries the cinema, radio and television have too frequently become instruments not of wholesome pleasure, instruction and the spreading of truth, but of errors, deception, and lies, he must exhort men to use these marvelous new means of man's genius as bearers of light, peace, goodness, and virtue.

Besides being a teacher, he must also be a *pastor* of souls and alive to all forms of suffering and ever ready to furnish the comforts which Christian charity can alone provide.

Habemus Papam

He must be not only a teacher and pastor, but also a *father*. When a new supreme pontiff is chosen, his heart inflamed with love must beat with particular tenderness for the peoples oppressed by an absolute, tyrannical and persecuting power; and likewise for all those social classes which still find themselves in straitened circumstances and misery so that even with the sweat of their brow they cannot procure for themselves or their offspring sufficient food or adequate shelter. He must take to heart, as did Jesus Christ, the cause of the poor and the uprooted. The rights of human labor, which the supreme pontiffs have already solemnly affirmed in encyclicals and other documents, will certainly be guarded by him and made effective by every possible means.

May the new Vicar of Christ be like a *bridge between heaven and earth;* may he recall the evil and the wayward to the straight path, and exhort the good to even greater perfection. May he be like a bridge between the various social classes, causing a greater sense of justice to reign among them and a more ardent and effective charity. Finally, may he be like a bridge between nations, even among those who reject, repel and persecute the Christian religion, and seek to bring about among them that true peace which is the only source of prosperity, tranquility, and progress.

But it is not sufficient to have a learned pontiff, a pontiff who knows the human and divine sciences and who has explored and become skilled in the subtle reasonings of diplomacy or politics. These things are also necessary, but they are not sufficient qualifications. Above all, Eminent Fathers, there is need of a *holy* pope, because a holy pope may obtain from God even that which natural gifts cannot provide.

While he listened with head bowed to the address of the secretary of briefs to princes, a practiced hand with the elegancies of the Latin language, Cardinal Roncalli no doubt allowed his mind to wander over the years of his early priesthood, his experience as apostolic visitor, apostolic delegate, nuncio, patriarch, during which he had striven to be a teacher, pastor, father, bridge between God and men, for all. Moreover, the themes of the allocution heard on this occasion would again appear in his message *Urbi et Orbi,* delivered the day after his elevation to the pontifical throne.

In the afternoon of October 25, the cardinals again proceeded to the Vatican to enter the strict closure of the conclave. The first to pass beneath the Arco delle Campane of St. Peter's, at 3:00 P.M., was Cardinal Micara. The last to arrive was the Brazilian Cardinal de Vasconcellos Motta, at 3:15. The Chinese Cardinal Tienchensin had to be brought in an ambulance to the Court of St. Damasus, and from there reached his cell by using the elevator.

From the Sala dei Paramenti each cardinal, dressed in violet cassock and mozzetta, accompanied by his conclavists and escorted by two Swiss Guards, proceeded to the Pauline Chapel. In the Sala Regia, situated on the way, the Noble Guards were drawn up in two lines to pay homage.

After the singing of the *Veni Creator* by the papal choir, the procession of cardinals moved to the Sistine Chapel, preceded by the papal cross and the prefect of papal ceremonies, Msgr. Dante. The secretary of the conclave, Msgr. Alberto Di Iorio, brought up the rear.

When they had entered the chapel, Cardinal-Dean Tisserant recited the Collect *Deus qui corda fidelium* at the altar. Then, after the prefect of ceremonies had announced the traditional *extra omnes,* the doors were shut and a detachment of Swiss Guards placed before them.

In the Sistine Chapel the cardinals listened to the reading of the apostolic constitution of Pius XII, *Vacantis Apostolicæ Sedis,* of December 8, 1945, containing the rules to be observed during the election of the supreme pontiff. Then they took the prescribed oath, which was read out to them by the prefect of ceremonies:

We the cardinal bishops, priests and deacons of the Holy Roman Church, promise and swear to observe literally and inviolably all that is contained in the constitution of the Supreme Pontiff Pius XII regarding the vacancy of the Apostolic See and the election of the Roman pontiff, which begins with the words *Vacantis Apostolicæ Sedis* of December 8, 1945. Moreover, we promise, declare and swear that whoever among us shall be elected, by the will of God, to be Roman pontiff shall never cease to assert and to guard, wholly and strenuously, the spiritual and also the temporal rights, especially of the civil principate of the Roman pontiff, and the liberty of the Holy See, and if need be to defend same, and that after his elevation to the pontificate he shall make this promise again confirmed by an oath. Especially do we promise and swear, under the penalties provided in the constitution of Pius XII, *Vacantis Apostolicæ Sedis,* that we and also our servants or conclavists shall scrupulously observe secrecy with regard to all that pertains in any manner to the election of the Roman pontiff and also with regard to what is done in the conclave or place of election. This secrecy we undertake not to violate either during the conclave or after the election of a new pontiff, unless special permission or express dispensation shall be granted for this by the future pontiff. Moreover, we shall not accept in any manner from any civil authority, under any form whatsoever, the responsibility for declaring a veto or exclusion, even under the guise of a simple desire, or manifest such veto, however known to us, whether before the whole College of Cardinals, or individual cardinals, whether in writing, or orally, directly or indirectly, obliquely or by others, before the conclave begins or during the conclave. Moreover, we shall give no aid or assistance to any intervention, intercession, or any other means by which lay powers of whatever rank or order might attempt to interfere in the election of the supreme pontiff.

Fifty-one cardinals entered the conclave, that is, one less than the number that arrived in Rome. Less than two hours before the conclave was due to open, the archbishop of Detroit, Cardinal Mooney, was stricken with a heart attack and died.

The following cardinals were present in conclave: Tisserant, Micara, Pizzardo, Aloisi Masella, Tedeschini, Mimmi, van Roey, Gonçalves Cerejeira, Liénart, Fumasoni Biondi, Fossati, dalla

Costa, Tappouni, Copello, Gerlier, Agagianian, McGuigan, Roques, de Vasconcellos Motta, Gilroy, Spellman, Caro Rodriguez, de Gouveia, de Barros Câmara, Pla y Deniel, Arteaga y Betancourt, Frings, Ruffini, Caggiano, Tienchensin, da Silva, Cicognani, Roncalli, Valeri, Ciriaci, Feltin, de la Torre, Grente, Siri, D'Alton, McIntyre, Lercaro, Wyszyński, de Arriba y Castro, Quiroga y Palacios, Leger, Luque, Gracias, Wendel, Canali, and Ottaviani.

There were seventeen Italian cardinals, six French, three Brazilian, three Spanish, two Portuguese, two of Oriental rite, two Argentinian, two Canadian, two American, two German, and one each from the following countries: Belgium, Australia, Chile, Cuba, China, Ecuador, Ireland, Poland, Colombia, and India.

At 6:08 P.M. the bell in the Court of St. Damasus tolled three times, announcing that it was time to close the precincts of the conclave for the election of the 263rd[1] successor of St. Peter. Shortly before, the heads of the three orders of

[1] The exact number of legitimate popes is a matter of discussion among scholars, the Church never having pronounced on the subject (nor is it likely to do so). The above figure is almost certainly wrong, even though based upon the improved list prepared by Msgr. Mercati and now regularly printed in the *Annuario pontificio*. This list wisely neglects to number the popes, but falls short in certain other respects. A better, more scientific list is that of the historian A. Pietro Frutaz printed in the *Enciclopedia Cattolica*, 9 (1952), 759-764. According to this, Pius XII was the 258th pope; so John XXIII is the 259th. [*Transl.*]

129

cardinals, Tisserant, van Roey, and Canali, together with the Cardinal Camerlengo, Aloisi Masella, had been present at the barring of the two inside entrances of the area in the Court of St. Damasus and Borgia Court.

After the ceremonies connected with the closing were over, the cardinals retired to their cells. Cardinal Roncalli had obtained by lot the cell set up in the offices of the commander of the Noble Guard. The sign "Il Commandante" was still visible above the door. His throne in the Sistine Chapel was on the right of the main door between those of Cardinals Valeri and Cicognani.

THE ELECTION

On the following day, Sunday, October 26, after the Mass of the Holy Ghost, the first voting took place at 10:00 A.M. Michelangelo's enormous fresco of the Last Judgment was covered in part by a tapestry above the altar representing the descent of the Holy Ghost. By turns the cardinals went to the altar to drop in the chalice their ballot inscribed in Latin: "I elect as supreme pontiff the most reverend lord Cardinal *N*." Three cardinals chosen by lot went to the cell of the ailing Cardinal Tienchensin to collect his ballot.

As he came before the altar, Cardinal Roncalli knelt a moment in prayer, according to protocol, and then swore, as did the others, in firm tones: "I call Christ the Lord as witness, who is to judge me, that I choose him who I think ought to be chosen according to God."

The ballotings (scrutinies) were to be continued, two in the morning and two in the afternoon, until a majority of two-thirds plus one had been achieved for any one candidate. Eleven scrutinies were necessary on this occasion before the world would know the name of him who had been elected. For three days the Piazza di S. Pietro, bathed in the brilliant October Roman sun, was filled, at the critical hours, with thousands of people waiting for the signal of white *"fumata,"* indicating that an election had taken place. [Through inadvertence, or perhaps because of unfamiliarity with the new stove which had been procured for the occasion, the first signals appeared white when they should have been black and considerable confusion resulted (the Vatican radio even announced that a new pope had been elected) until the situation could be corrected. *Transl.*]

As soon as the conclusive balloting had taken place on October 28 at 5:00 P.M., resulting in the election—by unanimity, it is said—of Cardinal Angelo Giuseppe Roncalli, the cardinal deacon with the least seniority, Alfredo Ottaviani, called the secretary of the conclave, Msgr. Di Iorio, and the prefect of ceremonies, Msgr. Dante, to enter the Sistine Chapel. Msgr. Dante, summoning the other masters of ceremonies, saw to it that the canopies which had been erected over the thrones of all the cardinals were immediately lowered, except for that of the cardinal who had been elected.

The heads of the three orders of cardinals, Tisserant, van Roey, and Canali, then approached the throne of the new pope. Cardinal Tisserant, in his capacity as Dean of the Sacred College, put to Cardinal Roncalli the ritual question: "Acceptasne electionem de te canonice factam in Summum Pontificem?" ("Do you accept the election, canonically made, of your person as supreme pontiff?")

A deep silence reigned for a moment among the rows of princes of the Church, as they waited for the fateful reply. This ceremony is one that has taken place for centuries but always greatly moves those present because of its historical significance and bearing.

Cardinal Roncalli answered in carefully chosen words: "Hearing Thy voice, 'I become as one trembling, and fear.' The consciousness of my own poverty and insignificance suffices to explain my confusion. But seeing in the votes of my brethren, the eminent cardinals of our holy Roman Church, the sign of God's will, I accept the election made by them, and I bow my head and back to the chalice of bitterness and the yoke of the Cross. On the feast of Christ the King we have all sung: 'The Lord is our Judge; the Lord is our Legislator; the Lord is our King; He will save us.'"

Then the dean, Cardinal Tisserant, asked him again: "Quomodo vis vocari?" ("How do you wish to be called?") And the new pope replied:

Vocabor Joannes (I wish to be called John).[2] This name is sweet to Us because it is the name of Our father. It is sweet to Us because it is the name of the humble parish church in which We were baptized; it is the name of innumerable cathedrals scattered throughout the world, and first of all the sacred Lateran Basilica, Our cathedral.

It is the name which has been borne by more popes in the long list of Roman pontiffs. In fact there are twenty-two supreme pontiffs with the name of John, of undoubted legitimacy. Practically all have had a short pontificate. We have preferred to cover the little-

[2] This name had never been heard under the roof of the Sistine Chapel before. The last [universally recognized] pope who bore it was John XXII, of French nationality, who was born at Cahors in 1245. His real name was Jacques Duèse (Jacobus de Osa); a master of civil law at Paris; a friend of King Charles II of Anjou, he was bishop of Fréjus (1300), chancellor of the kingdom of Naples, and cardinal in 1312. He was elected at Lyons on August 7, 1316, after a vacancy of two years. Settling in Avignon, he never again left the place. He published the *Clementines,* the seventh book of the Decretals, and wrote or dictated more than 60,000 letters. He laid down the norms for sacred music in church; he enriched the evening Ave Maria with indulgences; he was a defender of orthodoxy and severe with heretics; he reorganized the papal chancery; he canonized St. Thomas Aquinas (July 18, 1323), whose theory that there could be no conflict between true science and dogma he approved. He founded a large library at Avignon and made the city a center of culture, as well as of government and commerce. He sought to improve the moral standards of the clergy and religious, and has gone down in history as an excellent administrator. It is not too rash to think that Cardinal Roncalli, by assuming the name of the French pope, wished to pay his respects to the Church in France in memory of the years spent in Paris as nuncio.

The John XXIII (Baldassare Cossa) who reigned in the fifteenth century (1410-1415) is not listed as one of the legitimate popes but as an antipope [pope of the Pisan obedience].

ness of Our name behind this magnificent succession of Roman pontiffs.

And did not St. Mark the Evangelist, the glory and protector of Our dear Venice, he whom St. Peter, the Prince of the Apostles and first bishop of the Church of Rome, loved as a son, also bear the name of John?

But We love the name of John, so dear to Us and to the whole Church, especially because of the two who have borne it, the two men, that is, who were closest to Christ the Lord, the Divine Redeemer of the whole world and Founder of the Church.

John the Baptist, the forerunner of our Lord, was not the light himself, but a witness to the light, an invincible witness to truth, justice, and freedom, in his preaching, in his baptism of penitence, and in the blood which he shed.

And the other John, the disciple and evangelist, beloved by Christ and his dearest Mother, who at the Last Supper leaned on the breast of the Lord and drew from thence that charity of which he was a living and apostolic flame until the end of his ripe old age.

May God grant that both Johns shall cry out in the whole Church for Our humble pastoral ministry which succeeds that brought so ably to an end by Our lamented predecessor of venerable memory, Pius XII, and that of his predecessors which were so glorious for the Church; may they herald to the clergy and all people the work with which We desired "to prepare the way of the Lord, straighten out his paths . . . that the windings may be cut straight, and the rough paths made into smooth roads, that all mankind may see the saving power of God" (Luke 3:5-6).

May John the Evangelist who, as he himself relates, took to himself Mary the Mother of Christ and our mother, support together with her this exhortation which is meant for the life and joy of the Catholic and apostolic Church, and also the peace and prosperity of all nations.

"My little children, love one another; love one another because this is the great commandment of the Lord."

May God graciously grant, Venerable Brethren, that We who have been blessed with the name of the first of this series of supreme pontiffs [Peter], may, by the aid of divine grace, have the same holiness of life and his strength of soul, that We may, if God wills, even be prepared to shed Our blood.

Immediately afterwards, the prefect of ceremonies drew up the act of acceptance, with the secretary of the conclave signing as witness.

Then John XXIII proceeded to the sacristy of the Sistine Chapel to don the papal vestments, namely, the white cassock with stockings of the same color, the red shoes with a cross of gold on top, the rochet, red mozzetta, red stole and white zucchetto.

His conclavist, Msgr. Loris Capovilla, his secretary in Venice, was then called into the sacristy, still ignorant of the election. It is traditional for the conclavist of the newly-elected pope to assist him to dress.

Msgr. Capovilla helped the new pope put on one of the white cassocks prepared in three sizes. But he did not, when he saw the calm face of his patriarch, give any evidence of that confusion of mind which beset the conclavist of Benedict XV, Msgr. Migone, who had to have his courage bolstered with the words: "Help me instead of crying. After all it is I who have been elected pope, not you."

Re-entering the Sistine Chapel, John XXIII imparted his first blessing to the cardinals. Then ascending the throne he received the first so-called "adoration," or obedience of the princes of the Church who, after kissing his hand, received an embrace from him.[3] It is said that the kindliness which the new pope evinced during this part of the ceremonial seemed to those present to be one of the most moving things about the whole election.

THE PROCLAMATION

After receiving the homage of the cardinals, the Cardinal-Dean Tisserant placed the Fisherman's Ring on the finger of the pope [who immediately removed it and handed it to the prefect of ceremonies to be fitted for size, in accordance with custom]. Then, preceded by the papal cross and accompanied by the cardinals, John XXIII proceeded to the balcony overlooking St. Peter's Square. Here, amidst the manifestations of joy and enthusiasm of about 300,000 people gathered there in spite of the virtual standstill of public transportation, he imparted his first blessing *Urbi et Orbi.*

[3] It is reported that John XXIII abolished the traditional practice of allowing the cardinals to kiss his foot before the hand on this occasion, a sign no doubt of the greater deference which he intends to show toward the Sacred College. [*Transl.*]

Several minutes before this the senior cardinal deacon, Nicola Canali, had appeared on the balcony and announced to the Roman people and the world the news of the election: "Annuntio vobis gaudium magnum: habemus papam: Eminentissimum ac Reverendissimum Dominum, Dominum Angelum Josephum S. R. E. Cardinalem Roncalli, qui Sibi nomen imposuit Joannem XXIII." (I announce to you a great joy: we have a pope: the most eminent and reverend Lord Cardinal Roncalli, who has chosen the name of John XXIII.)

It was now 6:05 P.M. on October 28.

The Church had its *Pastor et Nauta*, according to the legendary prophecy of St. Malachy.[4]

The first telegrams were now going out from the telegraph office of Vatican City to heads of state and governments, the secretary-general of the United Nations, apostolic nuncios and delegates, notifying them officially of the happy event.

[4] A spurious list concocted by supporters of Cardinal Simoncelli, designed to influence the election of 1590 in his favor. The plot failed, for Gregory XIV was elected instead. The mottos fit the popes prior to that time perfectly since they were based upon the histories and studies of Platina, Panvinio, etc., but become mere guesswork thereafter. No harm is done in quoting this so-called "prophecy," provided one realizes what it is, namely a piece of partisan electioneering with no basis in fact whatsoever. [*Transl.*]

7. His Message "Urbi et Orbi"

✤ ✤ ✤

THE DAY after his elevation to the pontifical throne, on October 29, 1958, John XXIII delivered his first message to Rome and the world.

Composed by the pope during the night which followed his election, this document reveals a great deal of the personality and spirituality of the new pope by its flowing style, its clear imagery, and frequent allusions to Holy Scripture.

The message is entirely pervaded by apostolic solicitude for the "service of God." There is no trace in it of the politician, sociologist, economist, nor of the theologian; it is intended as a message of pure universal paternalism and apostolic dedication. Perhaps that is why it has been said that the message is one which all can accept, even the declared enemies of God and the Church.

His first message also reveals John XXIII as a man who wastes no time over words. A few lines suffice to deal with great themes: his predecessor "of immortal memory" who had served the Catholic Church so well; his own person sustained by the power of God; the Sacred College with some of the cardinals regretfully absent; the bishops of the whole world; the priests, missionaries, Catholic Action; all the faithful, especially the poor; the flock of God deprived of freedom; the rights of the Church "rashly trampled on"; the Western and Eastern Church; the separated Christian churches; the welfare of less fortunate classes; the discoveries of our time; his dismay at disputes between nations, at the arms which are being readied as "instruments of death and destruction"; peace with justice and prosperity.

THE BURDEN OF THE PAPACY

"This hour of trepidation in which, through the mysterious will of Divine Providence, there has been imposed upon Us the very grave honor of the supreme pontificate after the death of Our predecessor, Pius XII of immortal memory, who served the Catholic Church so well, oppresses and weighs upon Our heart. We therefore raise before all fervent supplications to God, that He in His infinite bounty may give strength to Our weakness and lack of strength, illumine Our mind, and strengthen Our will.

TO THE CARDINALS

"We now embrace with great affection Our beloved members of the Sacred College, whose

140

splendid gifts and virtues of soul are well known to
Us, especially those among them who, with sorrow
we know, are far from Us and whose sufferings and
anguish profoundly move Us.

TO THE BISHOPS

"In addition We desire further to express Our
paternal and loving benevolence to all Our venerable brethren in the episcopate, who, throughout
the world, labor to cultivate the vineyard of the
Lord.

TO THE PRIESTS, RELIGIOUS, MISSION-
ARIES, AND CATHOLIC ACTION

"Nor can We overlook in Our memory the
priests who are the dispensers of the mysteries of
God, especially the missionaries, who, as heralds
of the Divine Word, spare no sacrifice in spreading the truth of the Gospel in distant lands; the religious men and women who collaborate in the
Church with enlightened zeal; and also those lay-
men who, under the guidance of the bishops, fight
in the pacific ranks of Catholic Action, and all the
others who, in whatsoever manner, aid the apostolic hierarchy. All of these and each one We bless
with an effusive heart.

TO THE POOR AND SUFFERING

"We pray to God for all sons of Christ, but
especially for the poor and suffering, and We be-

seech Him to grant to all in abundance necessary help and heavenly consolation.

TO THE FAITHFUL OF VENICE AND BERGAMO

"Among Our children particularly dear to Our fatherly heart are the faithful of the region of Venice, where We exercised Our pastoral ministry, and those of the diocese of Bergamo, where We were born. And if We are now far from them, We are nevertheless present with them in the charity of Jesus Christ, and We shall always be so. We trust, too, that their prayers, united with Ours, will rise to God to beseech heavenly graces.

TO THE PERSECUTED

"Our thoughts go out in a special manner to the bishops, priests, Sisters and all the faithful who live in countries where the Catholic faith has no freedom, or only in part; where the sacrosanct rights of the Church are being rashly trampled upon, where legitimate pastors are either exiled or banished or impeded from carrying out their ministry freely, as they should. We wish them to know that We share with them their pains, tribulations, bitterness, and that We implore the Lord, giver of every good, that He may finally put an end to such inhuman persecutions, which not only undermine the tranquility and prosperity of those

peoples, but also are in defiance of modern civilization and the rights of man, long since acquired.
May God illumine the minds of the rulers of those
countries, may He pardon the persecutors, and
may He soon grant better and happier times to
all those who enjoy legitimate freedom.

TO THE EASTERN CHURCH

"And as We do the Western Church, We embrace with equal paternal affection the Eastern
Church, and We open Our heart and Our arms to
all who are separated from this Apostolic See,
where Peter himself lives in his successors 'until
the consummation of the world' (Matt. 18:20) and
fulfills the command given him by Christ to bind
and loose everything on this earth (Matt. 16:19)
and to shepherd the flock of the Lord (John 20:15-
17).

"We ardently desire their return to the house
of the common Father, and We therefore repeat
the words of the Divine Redeemer: 'Holy Father,
keep in Thy name those whom Thou hast entrusted to me, that they may be one even as We
are one' (John 17:11). Thus 'there shall be one
sheepfold and one shepherd' (John 10:16).

"Therefore let all come, we beseech them,
freely and lovingly, and let this return be as soon
as possible, with the inspiration and help of grace.
They will not be entering a strange house but
into their own, into the same house that once was

143

illumined by the glorious teaching of their ancestors and made precious by their virtues.[1]

TO THE RULERS OF NATIONS

"May it be proper for Us to address Our appeal to the rulers of all nations in whose hands are placed the fate, the prosperity, the hopes of individual peoples. Why should not discords and disagreements finally be settled equitably? Why should the resources of human genius and the riches of nations be turned more often to preparing arms—pernicious instruments of death and destruction—than to increasing the welfare of all classes of citizens and particularly of the poorer classes?

"We know, it is true, that in bringing about so laudable, so praiseworthy an aim and to smooth

[1] This part of the message has caused a certain uneasiness, especially in Greek Orthodox circles. *Kathimerini,* a newspaper generally reflecting the opinions of the Greek government, recalled that John XXIII was well known to the Greeks for his charities and added: "He knows the Greek language and Balkan countries well. It would not be an exaggeration to think that the new pontiff will show a particular interest in Catholics in these parts, which will be well and good provided it is done with discretion and a scrupulous desire to abstain from any effort at proselytism." The independent *Vima* reported: "John XXIII is considered one of the Titulars of the Western Church [!] who are most familiar with Eastern questions, and one of those most interested in the expansion of Catholicism in our part of the world. This is a possibility which the Orthodox patriarch of Constantinople and the other Oriental Christian Churches, which have always been an objective of the papacy, should take into account . . . ."

144

the differences, there are grave and intricate difficulties in the way, but they must be triumphantly
overcome, even by force. This is in fact the most
important task, intimately bound up with the
prosperity of all mankind. Put yourselves therefore to the task with confident courage, under the
reflection of the light which comes from on high
and the divine assistance. Turn your gaze to the
peoples who are entrusted to you, and listen to
their voice. What do they ask of you, what do they
beseech from you?

PEACE

"They do not ask for those monstrous means of
war discovered in our time, which cause fraternal
and universal slaughter, but peace, that peace in
virtue of which the human family may live freely,
flourish and prosper. They want justice that will
finally reconcile the mutual rights and duties of
classes in an equitable solution; they ask finally for
tranquility and concord, from which alone can
arise a true prosperity.

"In peace, in fact, so long as it is founded on
the legitimate rights of everyone and is nourished
by fraternal charity, are developed the arts and
culture, the energies of all unite in productive
virtue, the public and private wealth increases.
The thought of great minds in this connection is
well known: peace is 'the ordered concord of men'
(St. Augustine *The City of God* 19. 13); 'it is
tranquility of order' (St. Thomas, *S. T.* II-II, 29,

145

1); 'The name of peace is sweet, but that which it signifies is healthful: there is a very great difference, as a matter of fact, between peace and slavery. True peace is tranquility in liberty' (Cicero, *Philipp*. 2. 44).

"It is necessary to direct our thoughts again and to consider with vivid attention what the angels sang over the crib of the Divine Infant: 'Glory to God in the highest and peace on earth to men of good will' (Luke 2:14). In fact, true peace will not be given to citizens, peoples, or nations, unless it is first granted to souls; for there can be no exterior peace if it is not the reflected image of interior peace and if it is not directed by this, without which everything vacillates and threatens to fall. Therefore only religion can nourish, strengthen, and consolidate it. Let those who reject the name of God, who trample on divine rights, and who finally with harshness seek to extinguish in the hearts of men sentiments of piety, remember this truth.

BLESSING "URBI ET ORBI"

"In this grave hour We repeat the words and the promises of the Divine Redeemer: 'Peace I leave with you, My peace I give to you' (John 14:27). And in the hope and pledge of this true and full peace, as of all the other heavenly gifts, We impart with ardent charity the apostolic benediction *Urbi et Orbi*."

His Message "Urbi et Orbi"

No less revealing of his innermost thoughts as he assumed the immense burden thrust upon his shoulders is the allocution which John XXIII delivered on the occasion of his Solemn Coronation in St. Peter's on November 4, 1958:

THE VOICE OF PETER

"Venerable Brothers, Cardinals of the Holy Roman Church, Archbishops and Bishops, whether here present or participating in spirit in this solemn rite which places the seal on the initiation of Our humble person into the great duties of the supreme pontificate; and all of you, Our most beloved children of every part of the world and of every rank of society, who, though occupied by a thousand cares for the interests of this present life, yet do not forget the spiritual riches of the life to come, toward which above all we must fix our gaze, We send you all Our greeting from a heart filled with paternal affection.

"We are gathered together near the most sacred memorials of the Prince of the Apostles, the succession to whose lofty ministry has been entrusted to Us; and it would seem to Us, in this memorable hour, that We hear the voice of Peter reaching Us, passing over the course of the centuries, as well as the voices of the two Saints John who were closest to Christ, and whose sweet and honored name it has pleased Us to assume.

We Have a Pope

"In these days of great mystery and trepidation, however, as We strain to hear the voices of the earth, while, on the one hand, We are comforted and encouraged by the universal joy and exultation which greeted Our elevation to the supreme pontificate, on the other We are made anxious and perplexed by the variety of the immense duties which burden Our shoulders: those duties, We mean, which are attributed to Us on one side and the other, in various ways each individual taking it upon himself to entrust Us with one, within limited horizons and according to his own personal aptitudes, his own experience, his own peculiar way of conceiving individual and collective life. There are, in fact, those who expect the pontiff to be a statesman, a diplomat, a scholar, an organizer of collective life, or, in short, one whose mind is open to all the forms of progress in modern life, without any exception. O Venerable Brothers and beloved children, all such persons are outside the right path to be followed, since they entertain a concept of the supreme pontificate which does not fully conform to the true ideal. In fact, the new pope, passing through the various events of life, is like the son of Jacob who, meeting his brothers in their human tribulation, discloses to them the tenderness of his heart and, bursting into tears, says: 'I . . . am your brother, Joseph' (Gen. 45:4).

148

THE PONTIFF AS GOOD SHEPHERD

"The new pontiff, We also say, incarnates in himself above all that splendid image of the Good Shepherd, as it is described to us by the Evangelist Saint John in the selfsame words which issued from the mouth of the Divine Saviour (cf. John 10:1-21). He is the door of the sheepfold: *'Ego sum ostium ovium'* (John 10:7). Into this fold of Jesus Christ no one can enter except under the guidance of the supreme pontiff; and men can securely reach salvation only when they are united with him, since the Roman pontiff is the Vicar of Christ and represents His Person on this earth. How sweet and how consoling it is to call to mind the image of the Good Shepherd as it is described in the Gospel, with such richness and tenderness of detail!

"Venerable Brothers and beloved children, We repeat to you as Our own the admonition and the invitation of the Roman pontiffs of every century, and in particular of Our predecessor Pius XII, of immortal memory, and on this avowal We wish above all to insist: namely, that We have at heart in a very special manner Our task as shepherd of the entire flock. All the other human qualities— learning, diplomatic perceptiveness and tact, organizing ability—can succeed in embellishing and complementing the reign of the pontiff, but they cannot in any way serve as substitutes for this. The central point, however, is the zeal of the Good

149

Shepherd, ready for every sacred undertaking, no matter how daring, straightforward, constant, even unto the supreme sacrifice: 'the Good Shepherd lays down his life for his sheep' (John 10:11). How beautiful is the Church of Christ, the sheepfold (cf. John 10:1)! The shepherd goes before the flock (John 10:4), and all follow him. If necessary he engages in combat with the wolf in order to defend his sheep. Then the horizon broadens: 'and other sheep I have that are not of this fold; them also I must bring and they shall hear my voice and there shall be one fold and one shepherd' (John 10:16). Here is the missionary problem in all its vastness and beauty. This is the solicitude of the Roman pontificate, the primary one, even though not the only one: it blends with many others of equal importance.

HIS MEEKNESS AND HUMILITY

"But of greater interest than mere action in itself is the spirit of that action. Every pontificate takes on a particular feature from the character of the person who represents it. And certainly all the features of all the popes who succeeded each other down through the centuries are reflected and must be reflected in the face of Christ, the Divine Master who trod the paths of this earth for the sole purpose of spreading His beneficial teaching and the light of His wonderful example. Now His divine teaching and His great example are summed up in His words: 'Learn of me for I am meek and humble of heart' (Matt. 11:29). Hence the features of great meekness and humility.

"Pious and fervent souls throughout the whole world, We beg of you to pray to Our Lord for the pope, with the intention of obtaining for him the exercise of perfection in meekness and humility. We are quite sure that many rich graces will follow from this exercise; and the continuation of the eminently spiritual work of the Father of all the faithful will render an immense service also to the entire social order in the temporal and earthly field.

ST. CHARLES BORROMEO HIS PROTECTOR

"Permit Us, finally, Venerable Brothers and beloved children, to make reference to something which is a matter very dear to Us by an exceedingly happy coincidence which touches Our heart both as priest and as bishop. On this day, November 4, which from now on will mark the anniversary of the solemn rite of the coronation of the new pontiff, the liturgy of the universal Church celebrates each year the feast of St. Charles Borromeo. The figure of this Archbishop of Milan, who is to be numbered among the greatest pastors of souls in the history of the Church in every age, always has been and still is very close to Our mind. It was beside the very precious relic of his heart, which is venerated in Rome in the church dedicated to him on the Corso, that We received Our

151

episcopal consecration thirty-four years ago. The life of Christ's Church has had its stationary periods and its revivals. In one of the latter periods, Providence reserved for St. Charles Borromeo the lofty task of cooperating in an exceptional manner in restoring order in the Church. The part he played in putting into practice the reforms of the Council of Trent, the example he gave in applying those reforms in Milan and in various other dioceses of Italy, earned for him the glorious title 'Master of Bishops,' as he was also counselor of popes and a wonderful example of episcopal sanctity. During the ceremonies of the solemn rite of pontifical coronation, it is permitted to add, in a special litany, the names of some saints to whom the new pontiff is particularly devoted. When you come to the invocation *'Sancte Carole, tu illum adiuva'* (St. Charles, help thou him), kindly utter with ardent hearts your unanimous prayer in favor and pledge of those graces which St. Charles will give Us, Our Protector as We now call him, and as he will deign to be for Us, now and always. Amen."

8. The Personality of John XXIII

✠ ✠ ✠

HIS PHYSICAL APPEARANCE

Aₙɢᴇʟᴏ Giuseppe Roncalli is 77 years old. Slightly less than medium-height in stature, he has a robustness of constitution which has come from his healthy ancestry and from having grown up in the freedom of the country.

As one looks at him, the first thing that strikes one is his high, wide forehead, with practically no wrinkles, his broad face, his rather light, well-shaven cheeks, and his delicate skin; his eyes are grey-green in color and he is slightly nearsighted; his nose is aquiline; his ears are large; his mouth has rather thick lips which, when open in a smile, form two deep furrows at either end. The tone of his voice is deep but clear. His neck is thick and of normal height, his hands large and strong, his fingers fat. His strong body and legs have enabled him to walk with rapid steps for considerable distances, even at his advanced age. This was one of the characteristics which led him, as a young boy

153

and in his more vigorous years, to love taking walks during his summer vacations at Bergamo, or to do so for the sake of mere curiosity and sight-seeing in the places where his assignments happened to take him.

His deportment is that of a prince of the Church.

Physical endurance is what has enabled him to grow up as a healthy child, adapt himself to the rather arduous life of the seminaries and, in spite of considerable physical discomforts (such as service during the First World War, numerous trips and residence in different climates calling for different living habits), to arrive at an active old age without suffering the usual jolts or manifesting the signs of infirmity.

The pope's health, in fact, is quite excellent. He has rarely had to remain in bed for any illness; in general, the only thing which has ever afflicted him has been an occasional chill without any complications, an indication of his strong constitution, which gives promise of a long and full life of work.

HIS CHARACTER

It is difficult to describe the personality of anyone, but the task is even more difficult when it is a question of some outstanding person who has been involved in many activities. In the case of John XXIII, however, the task of the biographer has been somewhat eased by the numerous testimonials to his character. Also, his recorded acts and words can be cited to illustrate salient features of his character, particularly with regard to his qualities as a man and pastor.

An open, affable, warmhearted man, John XXIII rarely fails to perform an act of courtesy, especially if he can please those who are working with him or for him. He shows the same affability toward all. Proof of this is the short conversation he had with two workers whom he met by chance during his walk in the Vatican gardens. On this occasion he also talked with some Papal Gendarmes, taking a paternal interest in their families, the towns from whi   they came, and their service.

He is humble   mes one who is serving the cause of God, but at the same time justly proud. "May I humbly present myself," he said to the faithful who came to San Marco to meet their new patriarch for the first time. He concluded by saying: "And these notes will give you an idea of the modest physiognomy of the man." Several months later, he begged them to refrain from any manifestation in his honor on the 50th anniversary of his ordination to the priesthood, except for their participation at the Mass "without solemnity" which he himself was to celebrate. Before the conclave, he wrote to the bishop of Vicenza, Carlo Zinato: "We shall be united in spirit, in supplication for me, *in timore et tremore*." And a few hours after he was elected pope he said to Auxiliary Bishop Olivotti of Venice: "Now we have to do the will of the Lord. . . . When one has put love of self behind one and is profoundly convinced of one's own nothingness and misery, then, whatever may happen or whatever God may decree, one is at peace."

When a bust in honor of Cardinal Jacopo Monico, a native of Riese, was unveiled at Riese in 1957, also the birthplace of St. Pius X, Patriarch Roncalli delivered a commemorative address before an immense crowd. What he said, and how he said it, his gestures, the way he behaved and talked after the ceremony, all this won the hearts of those present. The applause even drowned out the sound of the bands. Suddenly from a window, a shout was heard, higher and louder than all the other sounds and applause: "is Pius X, Pius X who returns!" Then all shouted in homage to Roncalli in whom they saw the saintly pope again: "Viva Pio X!" And the Patriarch—humble but at the same time an acute psychologist—thinking that it was above all with respect to his physical appearance that they found a resemblance, murmured to those nearby: "I am far different from Pius X; Pius X was a saint: I, big as I am, do not even resemble him physically!"

If he could not avoid the applause at Riese, he let it be known discreetly, before appearing in public, that he did not like it. And even at his first public audience granted to Venetian and Bergamask pilgrims on November 5, 1958, he good-naturedly expostulated with those who were applauding him: "Pope John dispenses you from clapping your hands, otherwise . . . we'll never finish."

The Personality of John XXIII

"A man of great goodness"—this is the way he is most often described by those who have had the good fortune to live close to him. But even one who has seen him only occasionally and enjoyed his conversation has gained the impression of a profound, genuine goodness of soul. His goodness is characterized both by the perception and delicacy of a gentleman and the intuitiveness of a priest; hence it is both apostolic and human, because experienced in the miseries of this world. As a man, Roncalli takes men as he finds them; as a priest, he is happy to be able to console them, make them content, correct them. Like St. Francis or Manzoni, he would make others cheerful.

Simple in his habits and manner of living, he knows how to make all those who are fortunate enough to be near him feel at ease, creating a favorable atmosphere in which mutual sympathy can spring up and grow.

Numerous examples can be cited of this genuine simplicity during his career as a representative of the Holy See, as apostolic delegate in Bulgaria, Turkey and Greece, and as nuncio in France. Other incidents are already being related of the brief period which has elapsed since his elevation to the supreme pontificate. It is said, for example, that the day after his election he called to the telephone Count Dalla Torre, editor of *Osservatore Romano,* and when the latter excused himself from appearing immediately on the grounds that he lacked a suitable frock coat, the pope chided his old friend: "We did not tell you to come in a frock coat! Your baptismal dress will do well enough and will be something to cover you. . . ."

To a group of pilgrims from Bergamo he said after his election, smiling amiably: "Do not be surprised if the pope is a little embarrassed, because many things in the Vatican protocol are new to him. It is not decreed that the pope must immediately lose all his usual habits." And he added immediately afterward: "Pray for the pope, because he has much need of your prayers."

On November 6, 1958, when he received the more than 500 journalists who had come to Rome from all parts of the world for the conclave, the pope confided in them with his usual simplicity: "During the last few nights in which it was difficult for His Holiness to get some sleep—a sleep altogether necessary, however, to make up for the fatigue induced by the arduousness of the last few days during which he was making, so to speak, his novitiate in universal fatherhood—he cast an eye over the many newspapers, not of course in order to satisfy his self-love, but because it is interesting to see that the world takes an interest in the papacy, and in order to know what was being said, for example, concerning the conclave. Well, this was the constantly recurring theme: to try and guess what the secrets of the conclave were. Of course, there were not two lines which corresponded to the truth. Even though the powers of journalists to see through things are remarkably good," the Holy Father concluded with a smile, "silence would have perhaps been the best policy to follow."

A logical consequence of this simplicity is the innate naturalness of his attitudes and deportment, which has characterized Roncalli at all times in his official career, so that it has never been possible to detect any sign of uncertainty or act of confusion in the course of ceremonies, functions, or speeches, however new or improvised or important they might be. Hence, to the applauding crowds in the Piazza di S. Pietro, he appeared completely assured, simple, calm, even on the night of his election. "It seems that he has always been pope," was the comment of someone among the crowd, "and yet he is just like one of us."

"True greatness lies in simplicity and in the feeling of God in things, . . ." Pope John XXIII would assert as he turned to a group of pilgrims.

His serenity, calmness, patience have their roots in a spirit of obedience, constantly preferred to every personal consideration. "What made me secretary of Bishop Radini-Tedeschi in 1905," declared the pope some years ago, "was obedience; what brought me to teach in the seminary, to become a spiritual director, to help the soldiers, was obedience."

Obedience is the motto appearing on his coat of arms as a cardinal: *Obœdientia et pax*. A student of history, he took the motto from an incident in the life of Cardinal Baronius who, going each day to St. Peter's for evening prayer, was accustomed to bow his head before the statue of the

Prince of the Apostles and kiss it repeating: "Obœdientia et pax." "If I see a cross before me," he said one day before entering the conclave, referring to the possibility, considered by him to be remote if not out of the question, of his own election, "I know that I must follow it to the end of the road, even to crucifixion."

John XXIII is a born conversationalist and pleasing storyteller, frequently interjecting anecdotes into what he is saying, and sometimes allowing himself to go off on sallies, gifted as he is with a typically Manzonian sense of humor.

"When he was patriarch of Venice," one of his nephews, who is now chaplain in a parish near Ravenna, relates, "after I had served his Mass, he told me that he wanted to serve mine, and when I protested, he said to me: 'No, no, I want to serve you myself because I want to see whether you know how to celebrate.'"

The story is told of his first walk in the gardens of the Vatican, when he met an officer of the Papal Gendarmes. Approaching him graciously and engaging him in conversation, the officer identified himself as a captain of the guard. "You are then much more than I," smiled the pope, "because I am only a sergeant," remembering the time when he had done military service with the medical corps as sergeant in 1915.

Broadminded, he is capable of showing, when there is need, an extraordinary insistence on justice, combined with fairness in judgment. That explains how such a humble and affable man may appear intransigent in the interests of good when confronted by certain situations.

With reference to his indulgent attitude toward both men and nations, and his natural inclination always to see the better side and find an honorable justification or explanation for every act or attitude, the remarks which he made during a private conversation to a young diplomat in Paris in 1952 deserve to be recorded:

The young diplomat—it is he who tells the story—in view of the cordiality and affability with which the apostolic nuncio had received him, thought he could "give vent" to a political observation. The diplomat was lamenting that there were nations who pretended not only to know everything but to have the right, as "leader-nations," to lay down the law to other people. And he cited one nation in particular. "These friends of ours," he concluded, somewhat carried away, "pretend to have been the teachers of everybody through the ages. They were not yet born, but they are convinced that they inspired even the Bible."

The nuncio smiled, nodding in a way that indicated appreciation of the remark even though he might have some reservations with regard to certain implications concerning a nation that was particularly dear to him:

"I don't know, really," he replied jokingly, "whether Einstein's theory of relativity would allow time to move backwards for those nations whose history appears later and whether they might not thus turn out to have origins earlier than those which are historically older. But what seems to me truly fine in the great nation to which you allude—I am a priest first and foremost—is that it seeks in the Bible reasons for its faith and inspiration for the principles which are at the basis of its dynamism and prosperity."

John XXIII has always shown a ready wit and ironclad memory throughout his life. "We Roncallis are all like that," his brother Giuseppe observed. "Angelo is able, now that he is pope, to remember a face he saw among the people when he was only a young priest." A keen observer of faces, Roncalli was fond of watching his peasant friends closely in the visits he made each year to Sotto il Monte during the summer vacations. He tried to remember everyone and to repeat his first and last names. During his last visit he happened to meet a person whom he thought he recognized, and whose name he remembered well. The latter stopped and kindly said that he was someone else. Cardinal Roncalli was not perturbed by this but said: "Oh yes, you are too young, and I too old. But I would certainly recognize your father."

His memory and wit aid him in his work. He never seems to tire and is accustomed to making quick decisions and rapid judgments with regard to the spiritual and material needs of men.

As he is naturally inclined to see the positive side of everything (he was known at Venice as the "Optimistic Patriarch"), Roncalli has sought throughout his life to inspire happiness about him.

Giordani photo.

Cardinal Roncalli shown greeting Cardinal
Spellman in March, 1954. In the center is
the apostolic delegate to the United States,
Amleto Giovanni (now Cardinal) Cicognani.

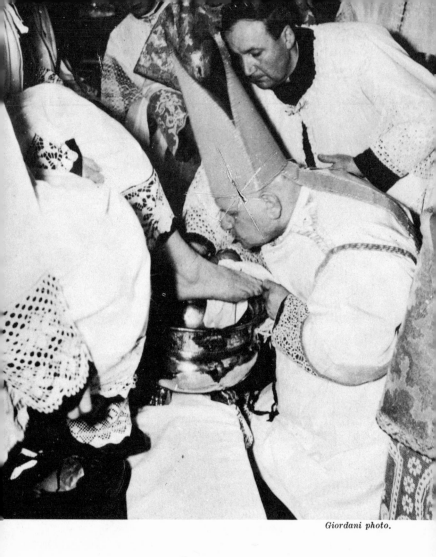

Giordani photo.

Venice. The ceremonial washing of the feet
in San Marco (Holy Thursday, 1956).

Venice. Cardinal Roncalli emerging from the
church at Riese, the birthplace of St. Pius X,
after ceremonies in honor of the saint (September 3, 1957).

Giordani photo.

Venice. The cardinal patriarch congratulates the winners of the regatta held on September 12, 1957.

Giordani photo.

Venice. Cardinal Roncalli voting in the political election of May 25, 1958.

Felici photo.

Immediately after his election, Pope John XXIII received the "obedience" of the members of the Sacred College of Cardinals in the Sistine Chapel. At the pontiff's right is Msgr. Enrico Dante, Prefect of Pontifical Ceremonies. At the pope's left is Msgr. Giuseppe Calderari, Under-Secretary of the Sacred Congregation of Ceremonies and Master of Ceremonies at the "obedience," and Eugène Cardinal Tisserant, Dean of the Sacred College of Cardinals. Standing at the foot of the predilla, at the left is Msgr. Federico Callori di Vignale, Prefect of the Conclave; Guido Gusso, cameriere of the new pontiff; Archbishop Diego Venini, Pontifical Secret Eleemosynary; Cardinal-elect Alberto Di Jorio, the secretary of the Conclave, who was elevated to the cardinalate immediately after the new pontiff's election.

Felici photo.

The "obedience" of Cardinal Spellman of
New York.

The "obedience" of Polish Cardinal Wyszyn-ski, the only cardinal from an Iron Curtain country who was able to leave his country for the conclave.

Pope John XXIII giving his blessing *Urbi et Orbi* after his coronation (November 4, 1958).

PIVS PP XII

One of the first things the newly-elected pontiff did was to visit the tomb of his predecessor, Pius XII. He is shown here at prayer before the simple sarcophagus.

Pope John XXIII during his first brief visit
to the pontifical villa at Castelgandolfo. The
pontiff, shown here accompanied by Com-
mendatore Bonomelli, director of the villa,
is standing at the desk of Pope Pius XII,
which remains as he left it before his death.

Pope John XXIII with members of the Vatican Secretariat of State. The Pontiff is shown speaking with the author of this book.

Felici photo.

Pope John XXIII entertaining prelates of the
Vatican Secretariat of State, following the
naming of Msgr. (now Cardinal) Tardini
as Secretary of State.

Felici photo.

Interior of St. Peter's during the Pontifical
Mass on the morning of Pope John XXIII's
coronation.

Felici photo.

On November 23, 1958, Pope John XXIII, as Bishop of Rome, took possession of the Archbasilica of St. John Lateran, the reigning pontiff's episcopal church. In the photo, the Holy Father is touching the keys of the archbasilica in a symbolic gesture of possession. Presenting the keys is Cardinal Aloisi Masella, Archpriest of the Archbasilica of St. John Lateran.

Felici photo.

One of the first heads of state to visit the
new pontiff was Prime Minister Roy Diefenbaker of Canada, shown here with Mrs.
Diefenbaker and a Vatican official.

The Personality of John XXIII

He wants to see people happy. A reflection of this innate optimism may be detected in his words as a teacher. Concluding a pastoral letter in 1956 on St. Laurence Justinian, first patriarch of Venice, he paternally directed the attention of his faithful to the following thoughts:

The life of everyone is beset with tribulations, but it is fine that what has been written has been written for our instruction, that by means of perseverance and of the consolations of the Scriptures we may preserve hope. It was St. Paul who wrote to the Romans, as he would write to the Colossians, with reference to the familiarity of the first Christians with the Divine Scriptures: "May the word of Christ dwell in you abundantly in all wisdom, instructing each other by means of the psalms, hymns, and spiritual canticles, sweetly singing to God in your hearts." This is the life and the joy of life: and such it should be for all of us, my dear brethren and sons.

And in the homily which he delivered at Lourdes in March, 1958, at the consecration of the great new underground basilica, he asserted:

I do not wish to attribute to myself any charismatic or prophetic gift by saying that since the inauguration of the new church the daily Eucharistic procession may take place without any fear of interruption because of rain or adverse climate: so ample is the canopy that it will protect every group and all the ailing who present themselves.

The entire world—nations and peoples—should take courage from this in the future. In order to make known that the way of mercy, justice and peace is open to all men of good will, the Holy Father Pius XII has recently exhorted, especially the young, with winged and fervent words, to be optimistic with a hope which does not cease to derive inspiration from the promises of Christ and confidence in the maternal protection of Mary of whom the mystery of Lourdes is an announcement and a certainty.

HIS STUDIES, LEARNING, WORKS

His love of study, and in particular of historical research, his teaching experiences, and finally his experiences as diplomat and pastor of souls, have made of Angelo Roncalli a man of wide culture, amply prepared to face the problems of the day.

Art, literature, history, with particular attention to that of his native Bergamo—these are the subjects he knows best and in detail.

John XXIII speaks (besides, of course, Italian and Latin) French, Bulgarian, Romanian, and Spanish. He has studied Russian and Turkish. He also understands, but does not have any fluency in speaking, German and English; and he of course knows Greek.

Always calm and spiritually edifying in his choice of language, he has the great gift of expressing his thoughts clearly and precisely, whether in his writings or speeches.

Numerous competent studies testify to his capabilities in the field of research and history. The most important, by reason of its subject-matter and length, is his work entitled *Atti della Visita Apostolica di San Carlo Borromeo a Bergamo—1575* ("Acts of the Apostolic Visitation of St. Charles Borromeo at Bergamo in 1575"), published in five volumes between 1936 and 1952. The idea for the work goes back to 1906 when, during visits to the metropolitan archives of Milan while accompanying Bishop Radini-Tedeschi to that city, he began to study the reports of this famous visitation. As he himself recounted, "The set of thirty-nine volumes bound in sheepskin with the title on the back *Spiritual Archives—Bergamo* immediately caught my attention. . . . I looked through them, and returned to study them in future visits. What a pleasant surprise for me spiritually! To find gathered together all these numerous and interesting documents relative to the church of Bergamo at a time so important for the restoration of its religious life, immediately after the Council of Trent." He decided therewith to publish the documents in a critical edition "with absolute scientific accuracy on the model of better modern publications of the sort."

The enterprise was warmly approved and was published in five richly indexed and annotated volumes. The work may be described as a political, religious and social history of Bergamo and its region, containing, as the learned prefect of the Ambrosian Library, Bishop Galbiati, points out:

. . . all the verbal instructions, decrees, and reports sent before the visitation concerning the institutions, disputes, abuses, denunciations, interrogations, processes, statutes and regulations; there are copies of the investigations, arguments in defense, discussions, memoranda, and sentences of the tribunals, of jurisdictional reports and disputes with the civil authorities; in other words, everything into which a bishop of exceptional energy would look who had been delegated by apostolic authority to make an extraordinary visitation to investigate an extraordinary situation. The documents speak for themselves, either reproduced in complete form or summarized, arranged in logical, chronological, and topographical order, and accompanied by notes which help the reader to appreciate the history of those times. The material is arranged in such a way that each parish or institution can find everything relating to it in one place, without having to search here and there for what concerns them. It is obvious how precious a compilation of this sort could be as an illustration of the episcopal activity of the great Borromeo in reforming the Church according to the spirit of the Council of Trent, for he was one of the noblest and most successful of the episcopal reformers.

In conclusion, Bishop Galbiati passed the following judgment on the work, which could hardly be surpassed: "I may be bold enough to say that, after the *Codice Diplomatico Bergomense* of Lupi, the present work contains the richest collection of documents for the story of the diocese of Bergamo."

This judgment was fully substantiated somewhat later by Belotti in his *Storia di Bergamo e dei bergamaschi* ("History of Bergamo and the Bergamasks"), in which he wrote that "Bishop

The Personality of John XXIII

Angelo Roncalli has acquired quite a deserved reputation as an historian of Bergamo . . . for his *Acts*."

Other important historical studies by Roncalli are: *Il Cardinale Cesare Baronio nel centenario della sua morte* ("Cardinal Cesare Baronius on the Centenary of His Death") (1908); *La Misericordia maggiore* (1912); and a biography of about five hundred pages entitled *In memoria di Mons. Radini-Tedeschi Vescovo di Bergamo* ("In Memory of Radini-Tedeschi, Bishop of Bergamo"), written in 1916 while Roncalli was a military chaplain. "These pages were written," the author notes in his Preface,

while war was raging over Europe, this terrible war which has cost so much blood and so many tears, and the material had to be compiled not in the leisure of the study but amidst the preoccupations of the present hour, according to the spirit of Bishop Radini himself, who gave to the Fatherland in its hour of trial the best that was in him, first as a simple soldier in the lowest ranks, and then as a priest, with the one desire to be able to contribute, in his humble way, to the comfort and spiritual consolation of Italy's valiant soldiers, to make the Fatherland truly loved, free, and great in the light of Christ. Today, on the second anniversary of the death of this venerable bishop, I place this volume as a wreath of leaves and flowers woven by pious hands on the austere grave where his body lies.

DON ANGELO RONCALLI
Military Chaplain
BERGAMO
August 22, 1916

In 1939, while apostolic delegate in Turkey and Greece, he published his *Inizi del Seminario di Bergamo e San Carlo Borromeo* ("Beginnings of the Seminary of Bergamo and St. Charles Borromeo"). Another work characterized by learned research and a sound critical sense is the recent publication of an ascetical work of St. Laurence Justinian, based upon a text he found in the Ambrosian Library while he was still a young priest.

Various monographs testify to the keenness of his mind and his deep learning, such as: "On the Fiftieth Anniversary of the Election of St. Pius X"; "On the Centenary of St. Pius X"; "On the Twenty-Fifth Anniversary of the Conciliation [between Italy and the Holy See]," etc.

Finally, as an indication of his culture and zeal, we may cite his pastoral letters, especially those on Holy Scripture, St. Laurence Justinian, his appeal to the clergy and laity,[1] his Easter message of April 18, 1957, and above all his *Trilogia Lapurdensis,* written on the occasion of the centenary of Lourdes. The Synodical Acts, including five masterly speeches he delivered in Venice, are now being prepared for publication.

We must also remember his many speeches as cardinal which were given considerable publicity, for example, his funeral eulogy for Cardinal Schuster of Milan; the homily which he delivered

[1] This letter, published on August 12, 1956, is a clear and decisive warning against ideological confusion, directed especially at the young who are so easily influenced, pointing out to them the proper way to follow: "all must work together, in unity of spirit, in the Christian bond of peace."

in the cathedral of Verona during the last Eucharistic Congress there; and numerous letters which reveal his kindness of soul, grasp of the problems of the day, and the keenness of his reasoning powers and diplomatic skill.

Among all these we may cite as an example the letter he sent to the Hon. Giorgio La Pira, in September, 1958, in connection with the "Mediterranean Conversations" at Florence, which turned out to be rather stormy because of the simultaneous presence there of Arabs, Israelis, French, and Algerians. "I may say with confidence," wrote the patriarch of Venice to La Pira who had invited him to attend the meetings, "that ever since the Lord directed my steps onto the paths of the world to meet men and peoples of such different inspiration and civilization from the Christian, something that has always been a great joy to us, I have divided the 'hours' of the Breviary in such a way as to embrace in my priestly, public, and official supplication, both the East and the West. . . . This is enough to indicate our good intentions, my dear Professor La Pira, and my participation in your efforts as a true apostolate. . . ."

A scholar and a humanist without being pedantic, his library reveals his broad cultural interests. On the shelves, as someone noted who happened to visit it in the patriarchate at Venice, are to be found religious works for the most part, especially in theology and patristics, and the large tomes of which he himself was the author dedicated to the visitation of St. Charles in Bergamo.

169

But other works of a cultural nature are not lacking, such as, for example, the works of Bossuet, the recent book by Jim Bishop, *The Day Christ Died*, a history of Venice, a biography of the doge Niccolò Contarini, some volumes in the collection *La Pléiade*, in which are to be found such authors as Rimbaud and Molière, and, strangely enough (but not really so in view of his wide interests and frequent travels) tourist guides to Venice, Greece, and Spain. Latin, Italian, and French are the predominant languages of the books in his library.

As an ardent lover of books, he has taken advantage of his numerous journeys and missions abroad to cultivate this inclination. His never-forgotten native country has also profited by his love of rare and beautiful books: thanks to the *bibliophilia* of Roncalli a rare codex with miniatures, which in the past had belonged to the Monastery of Santa Grata (Bergamo), was able to find its way back to its rightful home.

In 1945, while he was nuncio in Paris, he was looking at a valuable item which was on sale in a Paris antiquarian bookstore for 400,000 francs. Turning over the pages, the Nuncio, in addition to being struck by the beauty of the typography and the miniatures, was greatly surprised to see a picture of the patron of Bergamo and other saints well known because of the cult given them in the diocese. But the picture of St. Grata convinced him, together with other data, that the *Hymnarium* in question came from Bergamo, and he decided to acquire it. Two Bergamask residents of Paris generously came to his assistance, and the volume was restored to the artistic heritage of the city, a heritage as dear to them as to their illustrious co-citizen, the apostolic nuncio.

At Venice, as well as at Sofia, Constantinople, Athens, and Paris, men of letters and artists found in Angelo Roncalli a man who sought to keep abreast, to the extent that the responsibilities of his office permitted, of every cultural and artistic movement.

We have already mentioned, in speaking of his years at Venice, his love of music [2] and the arts, and his desire for improvements in this field. We should also mention here the interest he has always had in following the cinema, particularly in connection with the "Rassegna di Arte Cinemato-grafica" which is held each year at the Lido in Venice. One who did not disdain while at Paris to go to a good philharmonic concert, or conversed with Thomas Mann, or invited François Mauriac, Daniel-Rops or the painter Severini to lunch, soon learned to take an interest as patriarch of Venice—in a purely personal way—in questions relating to the movie industry, and particularly, in the souls of those who live in that world.

During the "Rassegna" of 1958 he invited, as he had on other such occasions each year, prominent personalities to San Marco for the inauguration of the new organ and had the music of Vivaldi per-

[2] Wolfgang Amadeus Mozart, Ludwig van Beethoven, and Johannes Brahms are his three favorite composers.

formed for them with voices and instruments from the Conservatory Benedetto Marcello, as well as by the "Virtuosi di Roma."

In the address which he delivered during the "cinema Mass," he pointed out, for the benefit of those present, the mutual influence of religion and art in the Christian civilization of Venice; he drew attention to the "catechism of the muses" in the symbolism and frescoes of the basilica; he found a parallel between architecture and the art of the cinema, defining the true function of the latter in these words: "To instruct, to educate, to amuse and to divert"; he pointed out the pernicious influence that was directly traceable to bad private lives or to evil living as portrayed in the films. After pointing to the advantages of a sound, useful, and noble art of the cinema, the patriarch reminded his audience that on the right side of the Basilica of San Marco, near the Porta della Carta leading to the Palazzo Ducale, there is a crudely sculptured twelfth-century inscription with the words: "Man should think of what he does, and consider that which may happen to him." "Gentlemen and brethren," continued the patriarch, "this warning was written for the Venetians of the twelfth century, who hastened to their tasks as supreme rulers of the state to the sound of the *Marangona* or *Trotteria,* but the motto is as good today as it was then. Since there is an element of tenderness in this crudely sculptured piece of laconic advice, I commend it to your artistic sensibility as men of the arts, as a simple, warmhearted recollec-

172

tion of this prayerful gathering in San Marco. Here the golden shower from on high is a delight and encouragement to the soul, summoning it, at all times and under all circumstances, to its highest function of informing matter and giving it dignity, nobility, and beauty. Amen."

HIS PRIVATE LIFE

The new pope is a man of simple habits and a rather austere mode of living, two characteristics which he has always had. He wakes up at dawn and his day is generally divided between the many activities of his office, prayer, and reading, at least to the extent possible. A brief noonday repose prepares his mind and body for the further tasks of the afternoon. In the evening, he generally finds time for quiet reading, since reading is for him a real relaxation.

Certain incidents, which became known soon after his elevation to the supreme pontificate, have confirmed the accuracy of this estimate. The day following his election the pope summoned Count Dalla Torre to the telephone at 6:45 A.M. and asked him to come to him immediately. The evening of the same day he expressed the desire to take walks, promising frequent visits to the seat of the *Osservatore Romano* in Vatican City. When Monsignor Tardini was named Pro-Secretary of State [3] the pope confided in him: "It would please

[3] Since Tardini was not yet a cardinal [he was named cardinal and Secretary of State in the consistory of Nov. 17, 1958],

me very much to stroll outside the walls of Vatican City once in a while, in the streets of Rome . . . but I am afraid that it would be impossible."

John XXIII, however, is not a creature of habit. His former diplomatic and pastoral activity has made him used to a certain elasticity of schedule, so that the routine mentioned above is not always strictly observed. He loves, as a matter of fact, to do things on the spur of the moment: thus he made an unannounced visit to Vatican Radio on the afternoon of his election. Great excitement reigned among those present who were not accustomed to these sudden and informal visits; but the pope spoke to them with his usual kindliness for almost three-quarters of an hour, chatting with all the employees in the station "in order to get to know them." Then he went on foot to the grotto of Lourdes in the Vatican gardens, where he waited for his automobile.

---

practice required that his title be that of Pro-Secretary of State. Monsignor Merry del Val, who had been Secretary of the Conclave which resulted in the election of Pius X in 1903, was also appointed Pro-Secretary of State until his elevation to the cardinalate. Pro-Secretaries have also been appointed when the Secretary of State has had to limit his activities or been impeded in exercising them altogether, as when Napoleon objected to Cardinal Consalvi and his place had to be taken by Cardinal Pacca. Pius XII never appointed a successor to Cardinal Maglione, who died in 1944, but contented himself with appointing Monsignors Montini and Tardini as Pro-Secretaries of State, of the second and first section of the secretariat, respectively. Monsignor Tardini was appointed Pro-Secretary by John XXIII (November, 1958) for the whole Secretariat of State [and has now been named Secretary of State].

174

The Personality of John XXIII

A particular gift which John XXIII enjoys, despite his advanced years and occasional departures from schedule, is the ease with which he goes to sleep, almost at will.

He is sparing in his diet, and as a precautionary measure eats only light foods, avoiding things that are too fattening, with the result that he enjoys unusually good health.

A glimpse inside the villa that he rented from the Barons Scotti in Sotto il Monte, in which to spend his summer vacations each year, will give us some idea about his personal tastes and habits. The official residences of diplomats, even after a long stay in one place, never give us an adequate idea of their personality. In the Sotto il Monte villa we see books for study, prayer books (some of considerable value), paintings, and objects of a religious nature. Of great value is a case in which are kept the white *zucchetto* of St. Pius X and the violet one of Bishop Radini-Tedeschi. There are pictures of his parents and friends, and mementos of his missionary tours in foreign lands. Now, no doubt, all these books and mementos will be sent to Rome. His personal library will then comprise, with the many volumes which he had with him in Venice, a considerable collection of works in various languages, from those of a religious or historical nature to the *Divine Comedy* and his favorite Manzoni, as well as poetry and modern novels.

His study at Venice was bright and was furnished simply but in good taste. The patriarch left it in perfect order before leaving for the conclave, with no unfinished business. Cardinal Roncalli always conducted his affairs in this way, even if he was to be absent for only a short time. Photographs of Pius X and Pius XII, together with pictures of a religious nature, adorned the walls. In his bedroom the same simplicity was to be seen. Beside his bed was a *prie-dieu* with a crucifix above it and a reproduction of the "Madonna of the Chair" by Raphael. The wall opposite the head of the bed was arranged with pictures of his friends: a big enlargement of a photograph of the cardinal with his brothers and then, in a row between the window and the cornice, photographs of his nephews and friends.

Two Sisters of the Congregation of the Poor of the Palazzolo will take care of his private apartment in the Vatican and his private chapel, as they did in Venice.[4]

The pope feels himself bound by strong ties of affection to his relatives and has a strong feeling for his native soil. "He is good, infinitely good," declared his niece Enrica, with whom he fre-

---

[4] The apartment is the same one occupied by Pius XII on the third floor of the residential part of the Vatican Palace. It consists of twenty-two rooms, including guest rooms and servants' quarters. The rooms actually used by the pope are: his bedroom (the one used by Pius XII), a large study painted in sepia, and a small private chapel painted light green. Two windows of this private suite look out over Bernini's Colonnade, while a third—from which Pius XII used to bless the crowds in the square—overlooks the Piazza di San Pietro.

quently corresponds. She has always joined him during the many years when he passed his vacations in the Villa Scotti in July or August. He would have supper with his brothers in Sotto il Monte each evening. No words were wasted on flattery, however, either on his brothers or nephews; each has continued to live and work in his own way: all are farmers with the exception of one nephew, Battista, who became a priest. The latter has declared: "He has always been our uncle and we have never thought of calling him anything else. He always wished me well, but would not tolerate any airs. In introducing me to others he would almost never mention that I am his nephew."

The news of the elevation of Angelo to the highest rank in the hierarchy of the Catholic Church was received by his brothers with great calmness. "Just as he became a priest, so he became pope . . . ," one of them said immediately after the announcement was heard by his brother Saverio over the radio.

This bond of affection for family and native soil was so strong that it brought Roncalli back to Bergamo each year, as we have said, for his vacation. The annual return of Angelo Roncalli, who had become so famous and who came back, in simplicity and humility, to his own home, to the scenes familiar to him from childhood, always turned out to be a great *festa* for the small community. These were days of reminiscing and spiritual joy for all. The people sometimes saw him walking along the roads of the countryside leaning on a small black cane. He would meet some acquaintance, speak to him with his customary affability and without showing any sign of aloofness. He often stopped to speak to the children, for whom he usually had words of exhortation.

Roncalli made a point of manifesting his love for his native soil in various ways. For example, one was the establishment of an Infants' Home. For many years he had felt the necessity for such a home, but financial straits had never permitted its realization. The idea occurred to him to use the ground floor of the Roncalli home for the purpose. Once this act of generosity became known, funds began to come in from private sources, frequently through Professor Pietro Donizetti ("Pierino" in the letters of Cardinal Roncalli), a dear friend of his youth, now residing at Bergamo. He wrote to Donizetti from Istanbul in 1943: "The greatest desire of my life would be to leave as a memorial of myself in Sotto il Monte the Infants' Home . . . but, as you know, I am not a capitalist. . . ." Then he added, "Dear Pierino, keep all this under your hat." In 1926 he wished personally to consecrate the shrine of Our Lady of Redona near Bergamo—his first consecration of a church. Finally, we should mention the moving words of the blessing which he gave to his native country and the whole diocese when he was elevated to the throne of St. Peter, as well as the words, full of goodness and affectionate longing, which he spoke to the pilgrims from Bergamo and Venice in the first audience which he granted on November 4, 1958. He said on that occasion:

> This is the first time that I speak as pontiff. But a simple parish priest would not speak to you otherwise, since there is naturalness in simplicity and the divine in what is natural. . . . From all this you will understand why the name John has been chosen, the gravity of the task, the responsibility of a poor son of a poor country laborer who must now shoulder the great weight of the pontificate. But he does so with the ancient faith and ancient principles which are the foundation of the Christian life. I hear so many voices and you can well imagine my state of mind. But I hear inside me: Venice will see you no more, your country will see you no more. What would you have me do, the will of the Lord has been clearly manifested: could I say no? Could I say: I wish to remain in Venice, I wish to remain in Bergamo?

HIS PUBLIC LIFE

With mind and heart in unison and with a solid background of education, Angelo Roncalli was able to confront the various ways which Providence had in store for him with confidence and success.

In his priestly role, as a wise and loving pastor of souls, he has always kept before him the ideal of the good priest whose various experiences of the world and men have constantly refined his knowledge of the defects and virtues of his neighbor.

Rising ever higher in the ecclesiastical hierarchy, he has displayed remarkable activity in widely different fields, but is always animated by a paternal attitude toward those who come in contact with him through his duties.

As he told the faithful gathered in San Marco the day on which he entered Venice:

Since early youth I have always wanted to be a country curate in my diocese. But Providence willed to send me in other directions until I finally reached here. Nevertheless in the many missions which have been entrusted to me by Holy Church, in contacts with men of other religions and races, my constant preoccupation has been to play the part of a pastor, and I am content with this. . . . I shall be in touch with you, simply, not in any solemn way, quickly, silently. The manner of a pastor is this: to count his flock one by one. . . . The pastor goes before all, opens the gate, guides his flock to fruitful pastures, wears his life out on behalf of his flock.

The hand of Roncalli, however, could be firm. He was always a determined defender of the interests and principles which the Church could never surrender to the world, although at the same time open to ideas which were sound and modern. He had occasion quite often to take a clear and decisive position with regard to delicate questions, even in political matters. And he always did

so with the good of souls clearly in mind, exclud-
ing, that is, any interference or direct participation in purely temporal problems. "Do not look
upon me as a politician, a diplomat; seek in me
the priest, the pastor of souls," he warned his
Venetians from the start.

As a pastor of souls the patriarch of Venice
wrote and published in the summer of 1956 his
"Appeal and Invitation to the Clergy and Laity
of Venice," to put them on guard against certain
"opinions which are going about, and are often
affirmed with eloquence and decisiveness, to the
detriment of sound principles and clear political
thinking and action, that is, of the discipline
which should inspire the thought, words, and life
of every good Catholic."

In his "Appeal," the patriarch gave an account
"of certain intellectual and practical deviations,
which, like false money, for some time enjoy a certain credit and currency among some Catholics,
and then lose their value and are exchanged for
others, to the surprise and dismay of the simple-
minded." Deviations of this sort were: 1) a subtle
tendency on the part of humanism, either ignor-
ing or having only a superficial acquaintance with
the principles of the supernatural life, to consider
as of secondary importance fundamental tenets of
Catholic dogma. . . . From which there follows a
distortion of what is most important in life and a
placing of greater value on wealth and vain and
spendthrift enjoyment, which the world prizes
and exalts in every sphere: business, fashion, in-

sane or exaggerated amusements, etc. . . . 2) a myopic, lay conception of life. . . . 3) the appeal for full and complete autonomy and liberty of action in the political field vis-à-vis the hierarchy and other organs dependent upon it. . . .

In the same "Appeal" he underscored:

With particular bitterness of soul the obstinacy exhibited by some in maintaining at all costs an "opening to the Left." . . . Here we find ourselves confronted by a serious doctrinal error and a flagrant violation of Catholic discipline. The error is practically to share and make common cause with an ideology, namely the Marxist, which is a denial of Christianity and which cannot be combined with an adherence to the laws of the Gospel of Christ. Nor let them come to us and say that that this movement toward the Left is intended to have a meaning only with reference to economic reforms, because even in this connection the ambiguity remains, that is, the danger that the specious axiom will penetrate minds that in order to do social justice, to help the suffering, and to bring about respect for the tax laws, it is absolutely necessary to ally oneself with the deniers of God and the oppressors of human liberty, and even to bend oneself to their will! This is based upon a false presupposition, and always results in disastrous consequences. . . . To say that an opening should be made to the Left is to say that it should be directed to the friends of oppression, friends who are deaf to every regard for the spiritual order and are only concerned with an imaginary welfare of a purely economic and material kind, which can never succeed in maintaining itself, if it can ever succeed at all, except by war and blood. . . .

The Personality of John XXIII

As pastor, he gave his children in the diocese of Venice this moral advice: "The only way to be Christians is to do good." He repeated the idea when he visited the Mayor of Venice, to return a call which had been made on him by the Municipal Council (which also included communists):

Here [in the City Hall] I am in the house of all and it is well, because it is in this place that attention is paid to the common good. It is also my house: among you who work, I find myself at home, because only he who does good can be a Christian; in fact, the only way in which one can be a Christian is to do good. Hence, in this house I feel at ease, and even if, by chance, there is someone who says that he is not a Christian, he is, in fact, because he does good.

As bishop he always tried to direct his clergy toward the care of souls and charity, as the principal tasks to which they should address themselves as priests.

As evidence of his skill as an efficient organizer, we may point to his activity as a member of the Higher Council of the Association for the Propagation of the Faith, before he was summoned to enter the diplomatic service in which he so distinguished himself. We are already acquainted with the main lines of his career in this latter connection. It is sufficient to recall, briefly, the kind of person he was as a diplomat of the Holy See and the enthusiastic words with which his election as John XXIII was greeted by the

French press, as well as by non-Catholic countries
where he carried on his mission and where his
work is appreciated. He is an engaging conversationalist and an attentive and patient observer
and has the gift of winning over those who are
speaking to him—*"Une bonté envahissante,"* as
one French statesman put it. How many problems
have been solved in this way, without bureaucracy
and protocol!

He has always been a gracious host, accustomed to receiving guests from all ranks of society
at his well-appointed table, conscious of the importance of good food and wines as a tool in the
diplomatic trade. Also, as patriarch of Venice, he
attached an undeniable importance to dinners in
order to help create an atmosphere of cordiality
even among those who were on opposite sides of
the fence. (A Venetian prelate who was asked what
the pope probably said immediately after his election, replied, jokingly: "When it was seven-thirty
he probably remarked: 'It is now time to go and
have dinner.' ")

He would receive the persons who came to call
on him in his study by rising and then accompanying them to the door after their discussion,
whether as nuncio or patriarch.

Naturally sociable and witty, he has not laid
aside these amiable traits as pope. Stories are already beginning to circulate about this attractive
side of John XXIII. It is said that, in one of the
first private audiences he granted, he confessed to
the distinguished visitor: "The most difficult

184

thing for a pope is to accustom himself to all these people who are constantly about him." [5]

Sympathetic to progress and appreciative of modern thought (though always careful to point out its limitations, errors, and confusions), alive to all social problems, he has not failed to make his voice heard, calmly, sometimes with sorrow, but always in a conciliatory vein and with thought for the common good, especially for the lot of the less fortunate. With regard to his awareness of labor problems, his Christmas Message of 1955 as patriarch of Venice still deserves to be recalled with admiration. He had been reminding his listeners of the trials of poverty and unemployment, and continued:

The daily newspapers are enough to sadden the first hours of each day: notices of shops closed, or reduced schedules, or worse, reductions in the staff. With saddened voice I would like to implore all those

[5] At the Vatican he has kept his young valet, Guido Gusso, as personal chamberlain. When the faithful Guido responded to a call and knelt before the pope, according to etiquette, John XXIII said: "If you continue to do this I'll have to look for a new chamberlain. Let's pretend that we are still in Venice. . . ." The pope's custom of having tea every afternoon caused an English journalist to write that John XXIII has "certain British habits." The pope's comment reportedly was: "It seems that it is not very difficult to become English these days; all one has to do is have tea." The chauffeur of Pius XII, Angelo Stoppa, thought that he ought to hand in his resignation when John XXIII had been elected. When asked why he had done so, Stoppa is said to have replied: "I thought your Holiness already had a driver, and I am beginning to get old . . . ." John XXIII replied: "For the traffic we have in our State [Vatican City] you are not too old. Stay. . . ."

who have the authority and financial means not to try further our good people who are attracted by "fatal adventures" when they think there is a lack of good will, of courage, of a spirit of solidarity in helping them and saving them from despair. Ten, fifty, a hundred workers dismissed from offices and shops, recall to mind their wives, their numerous children, often old parents, plunged into despair. We all felt disturbed by this. I do not dare, I do not feel that I should say more, but I appeal to the managers of companies, to their technical and economic advisers, and I beseech them, in the name of God, to bear in mind that the intelligence and material prosperity with which they have been endowed were placed at their disposal not only for personal use, but that they might be ministers of Providence for the advantage of the human family. They should consider themselves dedicated to the arduous but very necessary achievement of a social service: to earn the title and distinction of those who work in the spirit of the Old and New Testament.

SOME JUDGMENTS

A short but interesting sketch of John XXIII has been drawn by Cardinal Montini, archbishop of Milan. The former Pro-Secretary of State, and as such in a certain sense the superior of Archbishop Roncalli as apostolic delegate and nuncio, gave the following account to a newspaper agency after the election of the new pope:

He is a most lovable person, and it is owing to his natural goodness of soul that a large part of his success as a diplomat is due. When he went to France as nuncio toward the end of 1944, the situation was very uncertain with regard to a large part of the episcopate. It was thanks to the apostolic nuncio that many questions could immediately be ironed out and that the appointments of bishops could be agreed upon with mutual satisfaction. The new pontiff is moreover a person of great culture. He loves study, especially history. . . . He is an able conversationalist, is full of a Manzonian sense of humor, and an agreeable storyteller who loves a good story. As a confirmation of the sympathy he won for himself in France, it is enough to recall that when ex-President Auriol came to Italy recently, he could not pass up making a trip to see Patriarch of Venice Roncalli. I should also add that the new pope has the tastes of a humanist and is very keenly interested in art.

Archbishop Urbani of Verona [now Cardinal Archbishop of Venice], who was in close contact with Cardinal Roncalli, his metropolitan as patriarch of Venice, has emphasized the happy marriage in him of the qualities of goodness, virtue, knowledge, and balance, revealed by Roncalli during his government of the see of Venice:

The patriarch was young in temperament, energy, ideas, programs. From the first contact with him he knew how to win the sympathy, esteem and affection, the admiration of all, clergy and people. It had become almost second nature for him in winning peoples' sympathy to use the arms of simplicity, frankness, amiability. Anyone dealing with him, even with regard to the most complicated matters, was impressed by his ability to smooth difficulties and reduce mat-

ters to the essential, and his quickness in pointing out
the most suitable and proper solution. No one ever
remembers having seen him angry, no one has ever
surprised him in anger with anyone, no one has ever
noticed in his warm and robust voice a tone of irrita-
tion or bad humor. This constant serenity of spirit,
certainly based upon a happy temperament and his inclination to optimism, appears to one who has known
him for a long time as the fruit of long training in the
virtues, the result of interior discipline, the fortunate
meeting of a lively intelligence with an ardent heart,
tenacious will, balanced character. His evident love
for his fellow man and a soul endowed with an appreciation of art, his innate tact and courtesy, his refined
nature, these are the qualities which have won him
the hearts of all who came into contact with him, even
if they had to be reproved for something. But he knew
how to handle things so that even the one who had to
be chided was not displeased. It is not a question of
weakness, overindulgence or a passive attitude; he
knew how, when the occasion demanded, to be decisive, firm, and strong-willed. But he always preferred
to strong-arm methods a long and down-to-earth talk,
which succeeded in bringing the person round to his
way of thinking almost imperceptibly: in short, an
iron fist in a velvet glove. Only exuberance can win
the hearts of Venetians.

9. Chronology of the Life of John XXIII

✠ ✠ ✠

NOVEMBER 25, 1881

Pope John XXIII was born as Angelo Giuseppe Roncalli in Sotto il Monte, in the province and diocese of Bergamo, to Giovanni Battista Roncalli and Marianna Mazzola, as the third of ten children, the first son.

NOVEMBER 25, 1881

He was baptized later the same day in the parish church of San Giovanni Battista in Sotto il Monte, by the parish priest Don Francesco Rebuzzini, having as godfather his uncle Saverio Roncalli.

1892 - 1900

After attending the elementary schools in Sotto il Monte for three years, he went to the episcopal Collegio di Celana, completing his early education at the seminary of Bergamo.

1900 - 1904

He was sent by his bishop to the Collegio Cerasoli in Rome, where he obtained a doctorate in theology at the Roman seminary.

We Have a Pope

August 10, 1904

He was ordained priest in Rome at the church of Santa Maria in Monte Santo in the Piazza del Popolo by Archbishop Ceppetelli, Vicar of Rome. The following day he celebrated his first Mass at the Tomb of St. Peter.

August 15, 1904

The Feast of the Assumption he celebrated his first Mass in his diocese in the parish church of Sotto il Monte.

November 6, 1904

He enrolled in the diocesan Congregation of Priests of the Sacred Heart. He made his first vows on November 4, 1912, and his perpetual vows on January 6, 1917.

1905 - 1914

Secretary of the bishop of Bergamo, Giacomo of the Counts of Radini-Tedeschi. During this period he also taught ecclesiastical history, apologetics, and patrology at the seminary of Bergamo.

1915 - 1919

Military service first as sergeant in the medical corps, then as Lieutenant-Chaplain in various military hospitals.

1919 - 1921

Resumed teaching at the seminary and was spiritual director to the Student House founded by him in Upper Bergamo.

190

Chronology

1921 - 1925

Named Domestic Prelate of His Holiness (1921), he was summoned to Rome by Benedict XV as President of the National Council for Italy of the Association for the Propagation of the Faith. Pius XI later appointed him a member of the Higher Council of the same organization. Meanwhile, he also taught patrology for some time in the Roman Seminary.

MARCH 3, 1925

Appointed by Pius XI titular Archbishop of Areopolis *pro hac vice,* he was named apostolic visitator in Bulgaria. Consecrated on March 19, 1925, in the church of San Carlo al Corso by Cardinal Giovanni Tacci, Secretary of the Congregation for the Oriental Church.

SEPTEMBER 21, 1931

Appointed as first apostolic delegate in Bulgaria.

NOVEMBER 17, 1934

Named apostolic delegate in Greece. On November 30 of the same year he exchanged his titular see for that of Mesembria and was appointed apostolic delegate in Turkey and administrator of the apostolic vicariate of Constantinople. He remained in Greece and Turkey as apostolic delegate until December, 1944.

JANUARY 1, 1945

Appointed apostolic nuncio to France, he presented his credentials on this day to the head of the state, Gen. Charles de Gaulle.

We Have a Pope

JANUARY 12, 1953

He was created a Cardinal of the Holy Roman Church by Pius XII in consistory. Three days later he was chosen as patriarch of Venice.

MARCH 15, 1953

He made his solemn entrance into Venice and took possession of his see.

OCTOBER 28, 1958

Elected supreme pontiff as the successor of Pius XII and assumed the name of John XXIII.

A NOTE ON THE TYPE
IN WHICH THIS BOOK IS SET

This book is set in Baskerville, a Linotype face, created from the original types used by John Baskerville, the eighteenth-century typefounder and printer. This type has long been considered one of the finest book types ever developed. The letters are wide and open and have a businesslike approach. The finer hairlines give exquisite delicacy. The heavier strokes give color and strength. The relation of the two in combination gives a brilliant effect and makes for easy reading. The book was composed and printed by the Wickersham Printing Company of Lancaster, Pa., and bound by Moore and Company of Baltimore. The typography and design are by Howard N. King.